Sartre

Sartre

David Drake

HAUS PUBLISHING • LONDON

for Sarah and Kieran
with many many thanks for
all their support

First published in Great Britain in 2005 by
Haus Publishing Limited
26 Cadogan Court
London SW3 3BX

Copyright © David Drake, 2005

The moral right of the author has been asserted

A CIP catalogue record for this book
is available from the British Library

ISBN 1-904341-85-3 (paperback)

Designed and typeset in Garamond
Printed and bound by Graphicom in Vicenza, Italy

Front cover: photograph of Jean-Paul Sartre courtesy of akg-images
Back cover: caricature courtesy of Mary Evans Picture Library

Contents

Introduction   1

Early Years (1905–1924)   7

From the École Normale to the Outbreak of War (1924–1939)   23

The War Really Divided My Life in Two (1939–1944)   44

Existentialism and Communism (1944–1950)   63

An Anticommunist is a Rat (1950–1956)   81

Marxism and Anti-colonialism (1956–1967)   100

May 1968, Maoism and Flaubert (1967–1980)   123

Conclusion   138

Notes   144

Chronology   152

Further Reading   175

Acknowledgements   185

Picture Sources   185

Index   186

Introduction

When I was living in Paris in the early 1970s, Sartre's name was everywhere. The sexagenarian philosopher and writer was still causing controversy – as he had always done. This time he had assumed legal responsibility for a Maoist newspaper which he sold on the streets, and he was involved in a raft of political campaigns and actions. In June 1971 Sartre and the novelist and journalist Maurice Clavel publicly backed Jean-Claude Vernier's initiative to found an alternative news agency, the *Agence de Presse Libération* (APL). In the autumn of 1971 I accepted Vernier's invitation to join the small APL collective. Although Clavel was often at the agency, Sartre was not. However, in January 1972, responding to a wave of prison revolts across France, Sartre and a few other intellectuals tried to hold a press conference inside the Ministry of Justice about the prison system. They were quickly evicted and decided to adjourn to the APL offices.

When he arrived for the press conference, it struck me that he looked older than his 66 years; and for a man who had loomed so large in French cultural and political life, he was also a lot smaller than I expected. Since the 'events' of May 1968 he had refused to wear a tie and was dressed extremely casually, in fact rather scruffily for a Frenchman. As I sat listening to his distinctive rasping voice, I was both mesmerized and intrigued. Most people who get involved in politics have a radical, youthful idealistic phase and then, as they grow older, become more conservative and pragmatic. Sartre's political itinerary was the exact opposite. In his mid-sixties he was even more radical than he had ever been.

I stayed with the APL until it was about to transform itself into the daily newspaper *Libération*, which seemed a good moment to return home. I maintained contact with Vernier and other friends in Paris and set about trying to discover more about Sartre. Most of all, I wanted to resolve the enigma of his atypical political evolution. I read Simone de Beauvoir's *The Prime of Life*, *Force of Circumstance* and *All Said and Done*, which I found interesting and certainly informative, but they left me with many unanswered questions. Nevertheless, Beauvoir's autobiography was a good place to start to get some understanding of Sartre's life – at least from 1929, when they first met. For his childhood, there is always Sartre's autobiography *Words*, though in this book he is deliberately re-constructing his early life in order to emphasize certain existential and Marxist themes. However, it is certainly evident that from a very early age he believed he was destined to become a writer.

This determination to be a writer was realized in a most spectacular way. After the Second World War, having started to make a name for himself in the 1930s, Sartre exploded upon the French literary scene. Within a few years he had – in a way unparalleled in France or elsewhere – established a world-wide reputation as a philosopher, a playwright and as a novelist (who would be awarded the Nobel Prize for Literature – and turn it down). Furthermore, he was recognized as a fine polemicist, journalist, essayist, literary and art critic – he even wrote a song for the French chanteuse Juliette Gréco (*b*.1927).

In the ten years from 1943 to 1953, Sartre published four philosophical texts, three novels, and an essay on literature, had six plays performed and founded a review, *Les Temps modernes*, which is still published today. No other writer or philosopher could match his output. No other man of letters achieved such recognition across such a wide range of genres; no other philosopher attained such success beyond the realm of philosophy. In addition, as he acted out his belief in *commitment*, Sartre used his fame more effectively than any of his contemporaries to support those whom he saw as fighting for a better, fairer world. He was the committed intellectual *par excellence*.

However, it was not always thus. One of the paradoxes of Sartre's life explored in this book is how it was that the man who was seen as the embodiment of political commitment after the war actually eschewed such commitment before 1939. He never voted, and despite spending a year in Berlin (1933–4) when Hitler was consolidating his power, he wrote nothing about the rise of Nazism. Nevertheless, Sartre's attitude to political involvement changed radically during the Second World War which, as he put it, *really divided my life in two*. What was it about his wartime experiences that led him to turn his back on his pre-war lifestyle and to begin to embrace commitment? How did he express this commitment in his opposition to the German Occupation and the collaborationist Vichy regime? Within months of the Liberation – with the publication of the first two volumes of *The Roads to Freedom*, the founding of *Les Temps modernes* and a public lecture on the subject – 'existentialism' suddenly became all the rage. Sartre's philosophy of existence was a significant contribution to the body of European philosophical thought; after four years of German Occupation, Sartre's philosophy of freedom struck a chord with the post-war younger generation and even provided them with a guide as to how to lead their lives. Sartre was thrust into the limelight, and articles about him and existentialism appeared everywhere, from the popular press to literary and philosophical publications. Although he soon had a following, he was also attacked by the French Communist Party on the Left as well as the conservative Catholic Church. In 1948 the Vatican went so far as to include all of Sartre's works on the Index, a list of books forbidden to Roman Catholics. In the popular press 'existentialism' was employed as a fashionable synonym for bohemianism and there were exposés of Sartre's unconventional, and for many, shocking lifestyle, especially the 'blatant immorality' of his non-monogamous, non-marital relationship with Beauvoir. Thus with Sartre's new-found fame came the notoriety that would pursue him until the end of his days.

Sartre infuriated those who believed in 'pure literature' by advocating a literature of commitment, as he made clear in the first issue of his review *Les Temps modernes* (October 1945) and most notably in *'What is Literature?'* (1947). He also gained more admirers and detractors as he used his fame to support left-wing causes and movements at home and abroad.

All of Sartre's post-war political activities took place in the context of the Cold War and, as he now described himself as a man of the Left, this inevitably raised the question of his attitude towards the Soviet Union and his relations with the French Communist Party (PCF). After several years of being savaged by the Party, Sartre became a fellow traveller from 1952–6, but by 1969 he was attacking it as *the largest conservative party in France*. He was broadly sympathetic to the Soviet Union but this did not prevent him from denouncing the Soviet camps in 1950. Yet despite knowing about the camps, Sartre subsequently visited the Soviet Union many times where he met Nikita Krushchev, gave favourable reports of what he saw there and only broke irrevocably with the Soviet Union after its invasion of Czechoslovakia in 1968. He also met Mao Zedong in China, Fidel Castro and Che Guevara in Cuba and Tito in Yugoslavia.

Sartre had a long and honourable record of consistent support for anti-colonialist and anti-imperialist struggles, notably during the French Indochina War (1946–54) and especially during the war in Algeria (1954–62), which resulted in him being castigated as a traitor by French conservatives. He was also a fervent opponent of America's involvement in the Vietnam War (1954–75).

Sartre considered himself to be a libertarian socialist. In the period immediately after the Second World War, he rejected the determinism of orthodox Marxism which seemed to him to deny the notion of freedom that was so fundamental to his own philosophy. But by the early 1950s he was drawing closer to Marxism and his mammoth work the *Critique of Dialectical Reason* (1960) was an attempt to integrate Marxism and existentialism and extricate Marxism from the impasse in which it had become stuck. Eight years later, France was shaken by the student revolt of 1968 and Sartre was one of the first intellectuals to come out in support of the students.

May 1968 was another turning point in Sartre's life. After reflecting on 'the events', he developed the notion of the *revolutionary intellectual*: it was no longer enough merely to declare solidarity with revolutionary movements; intellectuals had to get involved. This is what he set out to do during his association with the Maoists (1970–73), though his scope for action was limited by his age and poor health. He was also determined to continue working on his book about the novelist Gustave Flaubert and refused the Maoists' pleas for him to write a popular novel for 'the masses'. After the dissolution of the Maoist movement, Sartre continued to be friendly with its leading members, especially Benny Lévy ('Pierre Victor'), who became his secretary in the autumn of 1973. With the onset of his blindness, Sartre's increased dependence on Lévy made many of Sartre's old friends uneasy about his influence over the old man. Controversial to the very end, shortly before his death Sartre once again caused uproar by approving the publication of his discussions with Lévy. To many they appeared to be a negation of many of his long-cherished philosophical ideas and there were accusations that he had been hijacked by Lévy.

On 19 April 1980, four days after Sartre's death, as his funeral cortege slowly made its way from the Broussais Hospital to Montparnasse Cemetery, more than 50,000 people lined the streets of Paris to pay tribute to France's most celebrated intellectual. It is difficult to imagine an intellectual today in France or anywhere else in the world whose death would provoke such a response.

Early Years

Nineteen hundred and five saw the first mass uprising in Russia against the Tsar, the Japanese annihilation of the Russian fleet, and in France the establishment of a unified socialist party and the separation of Church and State. It was the year in which Sir Arthur Conan Doyle (1859–1930) brought Sherlock Holmes back from the dead, in which Albert Einstein (1879–1955) proposed his theory of relativity, and in which the first two British suffragettes were sent to prison. And on 21 June 1905 Jean-Paul Charles-Aymard Sartre was born in the home of his parents Jean-Baptiste and Anne-Marie in the sixteenth *arrondissement* of Paris.

Jean-Baptiste (1874–1906) was the youngest child of Eymard Sartre (1836–1913), a country doctor from Thiviers in the Périgord, in south-west France, who had married Élodie Chavoix (1847–1919), the daughter of a well-established local family. After attending the prestigious École polytechnique in Paris, Jean-Baptiste enrolled as an officer in the French navy, but in August 1899, shortly after enlisting, he contracted a fever while serving in Cochinchina, today a part of Vietnam. By 1903 he seemed to have recovered his health, and while in Cherbourg he was introduced to Anne-Marie Schweitzer (1882–1969), the sister of his friend and ex-École polytechnique student Georges Schweitzer. They married in Paris on 3 May 1904.

Jean-Baptiste was granted six months' leave from November 1904 and, having resolved to leave the navy, spent much of this time in an unsuccessful quest for alternative employment. In mid-May he was obliged to return to the navy and left Toulon for a tour

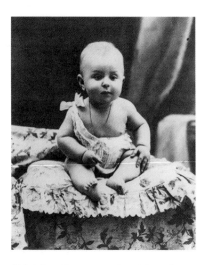

The infant Sartre was the object of an obsessive affection by his mother and her family

of duty in the Mediterranean. However, the recurrence of his fever forced him to go back to Paris in November where he was reunited with his wife and five-month-old son. His health continued to deteriorate and in May 1906 the Sartres set off for Thiviers. There Anne-Marie looked after her ailing husband with great devotion; so much so that as a result of her extended vigils and anxiety, her milk dried up and baby Jean-Paul was handed over to a wet-nurse. Despite Anne-Marie's efforts, however, her husband died on 17 September 1906. She was now a 24-year-old widow and her son was just 15 months old.

Sartre would say that he was indifferent to his father's early death. *This father is not even a shadow, not even a glance. He and I both spent a little time on the same earth, that is all.*[1] He went even further, describing the death of Jean-Baptiste as *the great event of my life: it put my mother back in chains and gave me my freedom.*[2] There is no such thing as a good father, he said, and had Jean-Baptiste survived he would have crushed Sartre and tried to control him. Sartre always maintained that his father's death was fortunate because it left him with no superego with which to contend. And his mother? She found herself penniless, with an infant but without employment among her husband's family in Thiviers. Deciding that she had no other option, she and her baby moved in with her parents in Meudon, a suburb half way between Paris and Versailles. The death of Jean-Baptiste left her a dependent young widow with a child, but for Sartre it meant there was no rival for his mother's affection, love and attention.

Sartre's maternal grandparents reluctantly assumed the role of parents once again. *Of course, families prefer widows to unmarried mothers, but only just*, observed the adult Sartre.[3] Anne-Marie's father Charles (Karl) Schweitzer (1844–1935) had planned to retire from teaching, but when his daughter returned to live at home, he decided to carry on. Born into a cultured, republican Alsatian family in 1844, Charles initially set out to become a Protestant pastor, but abandoned this path and moved to France in 1871 after the German annexation of Alsace-Lorraine, as did his brother Auguste who became a successful Paris businessman. A third brother, Louis, remained in Alsace where he became a Protestant pastor and also had a famous son, Albert Schweitzer.

Charles qualified as a German teacher and settled in Mâcon where he met Louise Guillemin

The theologian and medical missionary Albert Schweitzer (1875– 1965) practised as a doctor in the hospital he founded in Gabon, West Africa, at the jungle village of Lambaréné. He received the Nobel Peace Prize in 1952.

(1848–1930), the daughter of a Catholic lawyer. They married in 1872 and moved to Lyon, then Paris, where Charles established a reputation as a pedagogue, wrote several textbooks for teaching schoolchildren foreign languages and was one of the early pioneers of the direct method of language learning. His co-authored German reader became a classic and was reprinted many times between the wars.

With his long flowing beard and penchant for striking poses, Charles was both in and outside the home the epitome of the archetypal patriarch and Louise would often retreat into her bedroom to escape from him. *Charles inspired her with fear, a great deal of annoyance and sometimes with friendship as well, provided he did not touch her. As soon as he started to shout, she gave in to him on everything.*[5] Anne-Marie's parents treated her like a child, expecting her to carry out most of the household chores. The room she shared with her son was known as 'the children's room' and if she wanted to go out she had to ask for permission well in advance and be home by 10 o'clock.

Sartre's family was relatively privileged. *I saw society as a strict hierarchy of merits and power*, he wrote. *I was careful not to place myself at the very top since I was aware that it was reserved for serious, well-intentioned people who ensured that order was maintained. I placed myself on a small, marginal perch, not far from them . . . In this ordered world there were poor people, just like there were five-legged sheep and Siamese twins and railway accidents – anomalies that were nobody's fault.*[6]

In 1894 Captain Alfred Dreyfus (1859–1935), a French Jewish army officer, was found guilty of spying for Germany and sentenced to life imprisonment in exile. Following the exoneration in 1898 of the true culprit, Captain Esterhazy, the world-famous French novelist Émile Zola (1840–1902) wrote *J'Accuse! . . . (I Accuse! . . .)*, an open letter to the President of the Republic, in which he denounced by name the army officers who had framed Dreyfus. The Dreyfus Affair soon became a cause célèbre and in 1906 Dreyfus accepted a presidential pardon and was reintegrated into the army. He died in 1935, but it was not until 1995 that the French army finally conceded his innocence.

Sartre's world-view at this time was no doubt coloured by his grandfather's, which was underpinned by a belief in stability and progress. *Middle-class optimism in those days was summed up in the programme of the Radical Party – increasing material abundance, suppression of poverty, growing enlightenment and the multiplication of small-scale property.*[7] Charles was a progressive conservative democrat and a supporter of Dreyfus, although Sartre later regretted his not talking to him about this or any other political issues.

Sartre – or 'Poulou' as he was known at home – was a wonder-child admired by all, especially his mother and grandfather. He was waited on hand and foot and was convinced he was living in Paradise. *Every morning I awoke amazed at my happiness, marvelling at the sheer luck of being born into the most united family in the most beautiful country in the world.*[8] The young Sartre was adored, so he assumed he was adorable. He had a squint in his right eye resulting from a disease he contracted around the age of three, which left him with only 10 per cent vision in that eye, but he was told he was good looking and believed it. However, when he was about seven,[9] his grandfather took him to the barber's where all his blonde curls were snipped off. When he returned home, his mother locked herself in her room. *As long as my pretty curls fluttered around my ears, she had been able to deny that I was ugly. Now she had to admit the truth. And my grandfather himself seemed completely dumb-founded: he had gone out with his wonder-child and come back with a toad.*[10]

Sartre claimed, somewhat improbably, to have taught himself to read at the age of four by deciphering *Sans famille* (1878), a novel about a young orphan's adventures by Hector Malot (1830–1907). He was soon devouring volumes of his grandfather's *Grand Larousse* encyclopedia, and later claimed that by the age of seven had read Voltaire (1694–1778), Victor Hugo (1802–85), the dramas of Pierre Corneille (1606–84), *Madame Bovary* (1857) by Gustave Flaubert (1821–80) and other classics of French literature. It was in his grandfather's library of more than a thousand books, all neatly ordered, that Sartre *mounted his assault on human knowledge.*[11] As he added, *I never scratched the soil or searched for nests,*

The five-year-old Jean-Paul Sartre. 1910

I never collected plants or threw stones at birds. But books were my birds and nests, my pets, my stable, my countryside. The library was the world caught in a mirror. It had infinite breadth, variety and unpredictability.[12]

Sartre also adored children's magazines full of illustrated tales of stirring derring-do. In March 1907 Nick Carter, 'the greatest detective in America', made his debut in France and for the next seven years thousands of French fans, including Sartre, waited expectantly each month for the latest instalment of his adventures. This love of popular literature remained with Sartre all of his life and in 1963 he admitted that *even today I would rather read detective novels than Wittgenstein.*[13] He was also a great fan of the French adventure writer Michel Zévaco (1860–1918), whose tales were serialized daily in *Le Matin* newspaper and whose hero, Pardaillan, Sartre described as his master.

Despite this rosy picture, Sartre's childhood was an extremely isolated one. *Until the age of ten, I remained alone between an old man and two women.*[14] Around the age of seven or eight he claimed to have realized that family life was a fraud, a charade in which he was simply playing the part expected of him by his mother and

A day in the country, Sartre and his family in 1911

grandparents. *I accepted play-acting and insisted on taking the lead but in moments of crisis which left me exhausted I noticed that I had only a bogus 'solo role' . . . but no 'scene' of my own . . . I was giving the grown-ups their cue. Charles humoured me . . . Louise found in my liveliness a justification for her sulkiness, as Anne-Marie did for her humility.*[15]

In order to affirm his own existence, he turned to writing short stories. They were greeted with wild enthusiasm by Anne-Marie, who made copies and distributed them to friends and family, one of whom gave Sartre a small typewriter. Until his mid-teens, Sartre's writing consisted almost entirely of derivative cloak-and-dagger tales inspired by newspaper reports and adventure stories.

In 1970 Sartre told a biographer that he wrote in order to evade death: writing would make him immortal. In his grand-father's library he had discovered that great writers could live on through their works, which is why, from the age of about eight, he insisted on writing in an exercise book wide enough to sit on a bookshelf, with his name on the spine, alongside other authors.

In 1911 Charles finally retired from his teaching post and the family moved to Paris, setting up home in a sixth-floor apartment at 1, rue le Goff, between the Sorbonne University and the Luxembourg Gardens, and where Charles opened a language school. In 1913 he took his grandson to the Lycée Montaigne, informing the headmaster that the boy's only fault was that he was wise beyond his years. Sartre was duly placed in an advanced class, but his first attempt at dictation resulted in a paper riddled with misspellings. Charles was summoned and withdrew his grandson from the school immediately. Sartre's conviction that he was a genius carried him through this episode; he was simply *a child prodigy who didn't know how to spell, that was all.*[16]

Until he enrolled at the Lycée Henri-IV in 1915, Sartre had had little experience of school. While staying in Arcachon near Biarritz in 1914 he had briefly attended the local school, where he affected an attitude of superiority towards his classmates, and later spent a term at the Poupon School, a private institute in Paris, after which he was taught by a series of tutors who were eminently forgettable.

In his autobiography Sartre underplays his grandfather's role in his early education, giving the impression that he created himself. He dismisses Charles's input as little more than a few history lessons, but correspondence unearthed by Annie Cohn-Solal tells another story. In a letter to a friend written in January 1915, Charles wrote: 'I have made myself the schoolmaster for my little chap to whom I teach History and Geography while learning about them myself. Nothing is more delightful than cultivating and sowing seeds in this little mind.'[17]

Charles never missed an opportunity to poke fun at Catholicism, provoking, as intended, charges of being an unbeliever and a heretic from Louise, while Anne-Marie declined to get involved, retreating to her 'private God' who comforted her in secret. Although he was baptised a Catholic, Sartre's interest in religion was superficial and short-lived; by the age of eleven or twelve he had decided that God did not exist, a position from which he never deviated.

Sartre's mother bought him popular stories (a secret they kept from Charles) and it was she who introduced him to the cinema. At local venues as well as the bigger picture houses they watched melodramatic adventure films, many of their features borrowed from popular literature: the rescuing of damsels in distress, the dastardly machinations of the villains and the courage and daring of the heroes. In private Sartre would act out what he had seen and read or would invent his own scenarios – playing all the parts himself with the aid of a few props like a ruler or a paper-knife, though he didn't like being the villain: *I was always impatient to return to the leading role, to myself. Invincible, I triumphed over everyone.*[18]

One of Sartre's roles in the family was to defend his mother, who in turn assumed the role of older sister, companion and confidante. *The war years were the happiest of my childhood*, he wrote. *My mother and I were the same age and were inseparable. She would call me her attendant*

knight, her little man; I told her
everything. More than everything . . .
I used to trot along, looking tough
and holding my mother's hand and I
was sure that I could protect her.[19]

In October 1915 the ten-year-
old Sartre enrolled as a day-boy in
the Lycée Henri-IV, just round
the corner from where he lived.
He soon became immersed in the
world of dictations, rote learning,
multiplication tables and home-
work. In his first piece of work he
came bottom of the class, but by
the end of term his main teacher,
Monsieur Olivier observed of
him: 'Excellent little child.
Never gets the answer right first
time. Needs to get used to thinking more.'[20] At the end of the
year his teachers were all agreed
that he was an outstanding pupil.

The demands of school left
him little time to write, but
there were compensations. *At*
last I had friends. Me, the outcast
of the public gardens was included
from day one as if it were the
most natural thing in the world.
I couldn't get over it . . . I only
had one desire – to be part of the
group.[21] One of the most important friends Sartre made was

Paul-Yves Nizan (1905–40) met
Sartre at Henri IV and they studied
together at Louis-le-Grand and the
École normale supérieure (ENS). He
left the ENS for a year in Aden and
after graduating, Nizan, like Sartre,
became a teacher. He briefly flirted
with a far-right organization (Georges
Valois's Faisceau), then joined the
French Communist Party (PCF) in
1929. He became a journalist for the
Communist daily *L'Humanité*, stood as
a PCF candidate in 1932 and published
Les Chiens de garde (*The Watchdogs*), a
violent critique of 'bourgeois ideology',
especially its philosophical underpin-
nings. In 1934 he visited Moscow and
in 1937 became foreign editor of
another Communist paper *Le Soir*.
After the signing of the Nazi-Soviet
pact in 1939, Nizan publicly resigned
from the PCF. He died in action near
Dunkirk on 23 May 1940.

Paul Nizan, the son of a railway engineer.

In April 1917 Sartre's life was turned upside down by his mother's decision to remarry. She had first been introduced to her second husband, Joseph Mancy, through her brother Georges around the same time that she had met Sartre's father. Mancy was now a manager at the Delaunay-Belleville factories in Paris and had made contact with her again. Severely traumatized by his mother's remarriage, Sartre felt utterly devastated and abandoned. Mancy had stolen the woman who had been his companion-mother-sister for almost twelve years. *My mother certainly didn't marry my step-father out of love*, he stated in 1972. *In any case, he wasn't very lovable.*[22]

Sartre's sense of betrayal was compounded when, at the end of the summer, following Mancy's promotion to head of the Delaunay-Belleville shipyards in La Rochelle, he and Anne-Marie moved there, leaving Sartre in Paris in the care of his grandparents. In November Poulou joined them in a town he didn't know, far from his Paris friends, and living with a mother he felt had forsaken him and a man who had usurped his place in her affections. He enrolled at La Rochelle boys' *lycée* and did well there, despite the upheaval, winning prizes for essay writing and German, Greek and Latin translation.

His home life was another story. Whereas Sartre's grandfather was a man of culture, the man who had 'stolen' his mother was a scientist, a technocrat with little time for art or literature. In Sartre's view, Mancy was authoritarian, intolerant and narrow-minded. He tried to instil a sense of duty and respect in his stepson and talked endlessly of the responsibilities of the employer, though he had little consideration for his employees. Mancy's antipathy to the Russian Revolution (1917) was so strong that Sartre, without really being terribly interested in it, was persuaded it had to be a good thing. Compared to Mancy, his grandfather had been a true democrat and Sartre would later assert that his anti-authoritarianism dated from his relationship with his stepfather.

Mancy took no interest in Sartre's writing, convinced he was far too young to be dabbling in literature. *So he was the person I was always writing against. All my life. The fact of writing was against him.*[23] Mancy hoped that Sartre would become a teacher of mathematics or physics and insisted on tutoring him at home in these subjects. On one occasion, Sartre protested so loudly to being taught by Mancy that his mother came in and slapped him. *I got up with great dignity and went to my room while he scolded her. That was the last time she ever hit me. But it was all over. She had been mine, totally mine. Now forced to choose, she went against me. I had become a stranger. I was no longer in my home.*[24]

At school his relations with his peers were not easy. His fellow pupils were suspicious and resentful of this fancy, bright, imaginative Parisian, while his small stature (as an adult he was only five foot two) and his squint made him an ideal target for bullying. Many of the boys hung round the ships and sailors in La Rochelle, a port town whose atmosphere was imbued with violence. Sartre later stated that the boys, many of whom had fathers fighting in the First World War, had interiorized the violence of the trenches. In an attempt to gain acceptance, he would join his mainly middle-class schoolmates in fights against the wealthier boys from a local Catholic school, and especially the working-class pupils from the nearby technical school. This experience of *class war after class*[25] was his introduction to inequality and violence.

Another ploy he adopted to gain recognition was to join in the ragging of the teachers, especially a Monsieur Loosdregt, who was later the inspiration for a satirical story, parts of which were published in 1923.[26] Sartre told tall tales about himself and boasted about a girlfriend in Paris, but he was soon exposed as a fraud. Desperate to be accepted, he stole money from his mother to buy cakes for his classmates. Anne-Marie discovered the theft and Sartre's hope that his grandfather, who arrived in La Rochelle a few days later, would understand and support him, was cruelly dashed.

Around this time Sartre was further humiliated when he tried to gain the affections of a local 12-year-old girl. He approached her while she was with some friends, but she took one look at his squint and said: 'Who's this old prat with one eye that says "shit" to the other?' *I withdrew, as the group burst out laughing*, Sartre recalled. *I knew then that I was ugly. I had had such a hint after my grandfather cut my curls and my mother cried. But now I was absolutely certain: I was really ugly.*[27] 'In La Rochelle, Sartre thus lost his innocence: his mother, his privileged status, his precociousness, his prettiness, his centre-stage, his grandfather.'[28] La Rochelle had introduced him to violence, class differences, isolation and alienation.

Sartre continued to make satisfactory progress in his studies, despite playing truant and getting into trouble. However, Anne-Marie and Mancy decided to send him back to Paris, away from the rougher influences of La Rochelle. *She wanted to yank me out of that unpleasant milieu which she blamed for my truancy, for my lies and thefts. In truth, my hostility at home was mostly caused by her remarriage and her husband's stodgy character. That's what made me desperately seek my own peer group and, not being able to find it, to try and buy one. I never did make real friends. I never kept one.*[29]

In the autumn of 1920 the 15-year-old Sartre returned to the Lycée Henri-IV, where he was reunited with his old friend Paul Nizan. Both boys soon discovered they shared a passion for literature. At La Rochelle Sartre had continued writing cloak-and-dagger novels, but his reading matter was mainly 'women's literature' and adventure stories. Nizan and his more sophisticated Parisian classmates scorned such literature and soon, largely thanks to Nizan, Sartre was devouring modern French writers like André Gide (1869–1951), Jean Giraudoux (1882–1944), Jules Romains (1885–1972) and especially Marcel Proust (1871–1922). By now, Sartre was also much closer to his maternal grandmother, who encouraged him to read more widely: she recommended Stendhal (1783–1842), Fyodor Dostoevsky

(1821–81) and Count Leo Tolstoy (1828–1910), whose works they discussed for hours on end.

Sartre and Nizan were soon inseparable. *What mattered was that Nizan and I wanted to write. It was this that bound us together. The other pupils knew we wanted to be writers and respected us accordingly.*[30] Later Sartre claimed that Nizan was the more gifted writer, pointing out that because Nizan had remained in Paris while Sartre was in La Rochelle, he was much more integrated into his times. Sartre and Nizan decided to become supermen and Nizan gave them Celtic names: Nizan was 'R'ha' and Sartre 'Bor'hou'. Together they set out to explore the world. *We walked around Paris for hours, for days. We discovered fauna and flora, stones and were moved to tears when the first neon advertisements were turned on. We thought the world was new because we were new in the world.*[31]

It was in his final year at Henri-IV that Sartre, now 17, became interested in philosophy. He was convinced that a writer had to be a philosopher. *I thought that if I specialised in philosophy, I would grasp the totality of the world that I would talk about in my books . . . I thought that the point of literature was to reveal things to the reader that s/he had never thought of.*[32]

In the summer of 1922 he travelled to Alsace with his grandfather, where he worked on a short story, 'L'Ange du Morbide'[33] ('The Morbid Angel'), and a novel that remained unfinished, *Jésus la Chouette (Jesus the Owl)*. Both appeared the following year in a magazine edited by his friends (including Nizan) entitled *La Revue sans titre (The Review with No Name)*. The short story was a satirical account of a schoolmaster with aspirations to be a poet who seeks out the morbid and decadent, but eventually abandons writing, marries and ends up being awarded the Légion d'honneur, *the indisputable mark of the bourgeoisie*. *Jésus la Chouette* – published under the pseudonym Jacques Guillemin (Guillemin being his grandmother's maiden name) – recounts through the eyes of a pupil named Paul the tormenting of a teacher, M. Lautreck, who is eventually driven to suicide and who was partly inspired by M. Loosdregt at La Rochelle, although Loosdregt did not take his own life.

These stories show how far Sartre had moved from the swash-buckling, cloak-and-dagger tales he had written at La Rochelle. He had left behind the simplistic, Manichean world of good and evil, heroes and villains and embraced a more realistic approach. They also contain elements that were to feature later in Sartre's writings, namely a contempt for literary affectation, but most of all for the bourgeoisie, for bourgeois mediocrity, complacency and respectability and for the kind of self-deception that he would call *bad faith*. They are also very violent, which Sartre later attributed to his destructive individualism, verging on anarchism.

It was around this time that Sartre began to explore the idea of contingency: the notion that things happen, things are, without being a part of some greater scheme or project. Life, he observed, was nothing but contingency. He was struck by the contrast with what happened in the cinema. In films everything has a significance and contributes to the story, which has a beginning, a middle and a (usually happy) end. In life, on the other hand, there is no necessity. Sartre began recording his thoughts and ideas in a notebook he had found on the Paris metro.

Sartre showed little interest in politics at Henri-IV. He discussed the Russian Revolution with Louise and was stunned to hear her say that the poor had no choice but to fight in order to better their lives. His fellow pupils discussed politics a great deal and urged him to join the Young Socialists. He refused, partly because of a profound dislike of hierarchical organizations (which also led him, he claimed retrospectively, to support the Kronstadt rebels) and partly because he felt he lacked enough information about what was going on.

Sartre had decided to become a teacher like his grandfather. Charles had had a good life, earning respect and admiration, and there would be plenty of time to write. Accordingly, Sartre (and Nizan) prepared for the competitive entry examination to the prestigious École normale supérieure (ENS), France's elite teacher-training establishment. In preparation, they transferred to the Lycée Louis-le-Grand, which had a better record for securing entry to the ENS than did Henri-IV and which they attended from 1922 to 1924.

The Delaunay-Belleville shipyards at La Rochelle had gone bankrupt and Mancy and Anne-Marie had returned to Paris. This meant Sartre could now attend Louis-le-Grand as a half-boarder. He and Nizan performed well in their studies, although in March 1923 they had a violent falling out which lasted until October. In a text published after his death, Sartre gave a semi-fictional account of their relationship, which he described as *stormier than a passion*.[34] In later life he could not recall the exact reasons for the quarrel, but remembered it had something to do with the *Revue sans titre*. Throughout his time at Louis-le-Grand, Sartre continued to show no interest in politics. 'I never had the slightest exchange with him about political matters,' recalled one contemporary. 'For him at that time, unlike his friend Nizan, the world of politics didn't seem to exist.'[35]

In March 1921 the sailors of Kronstadt, an island fortress that had been a bastion of the 1917 Revolution, revolted against Lenin and the Bolshevik Party. At mass meetings they demanded new elections to the Soviet by secret ballot, freedom of speech, freedom of the Press for all left-wing publications and freedom of assembly for trade unions and peasant organizations. The Bolsheviks responded by launching an assault against the rebels, killing thousands of sailors, soldiers and workers who had joined them from nearby Petrograd. Others were executed by firing squad or exiled to camps.

At Louis-le-Grand, according to a fellow pupil, Sartre stood out 'through his hard work, his brilliant results, but also because of his gusto and good humour. He could already give you a little talk on boredom, and won over his peers with his sense of humour; he loved jokes and enjoyed ragging the teachers.'[36] In preparation for the entrance exam, Sartre and Nizan (now friends again) read more voraciously than ever before, devouring everything by the novelist Joseph Conrad (1857–1924), the poet Paul Valéry (1871–1945) and the philosophers Henri Bergson (1859–1941), Friedrich Nietzsche (1844–1900), Arthur Schopenhauer (1788–1860), Immanuel Kant (1724–1804), René Descartes (1596–1650) and Plato (427–347 BC). The results were published in August. Out of thousands of applicants, Sartre had come seventh and Nizan had also passed. They were both destined for what Nizan later bitterly referred to as 'the allegedly normal and supposedly superior School'.

From the École Normale to the Outbreak of War

While Sartre remained very close to Nizan at the École normale supérieure, he also made new friends. There was Georges Canguilhem (1904–95), another ex-pupil from Louis-le-Grand, who went on to establish an international reputation as a professor of the history and philosophy of science; René Maheu (1905–75), who became the Director-General of UNESCO (1961–74); and Raymond Aron (1905-83).

Recalling their time at the École, Aron noted, 'I cannot talk about Sartre without talking about Nizan,'[37] and in his autobiography he wrote that Sartre and Nizan enjoyed 'a friendship that was rare even among young people. Both were committed to literature and philosophy; both

Raymond Aron

were recognized by their fellow students as being special.'[38] Canguilhem confirmed this view of Sartre: 'First at the age of 20, Sartre was an extraordinary intellectual powerhouse which derived from his wide reading. And he had a lyrical way of talking about everything without any sign of self-consciousness.

After graduating from the École normale supérieure in 1928, Raymond Aron wrote a doctoral thesis on the philosophy of history (1938). In 1940 he joined General Charles de Gaulle (1890–1970) in London, where he helped to produce *La France libre*, a cultural resistance journal for and by French exiled intellectuals. Later he was briefly a member of the editorial board of *Les Temps modernes*, the review launched by Sartre in 1945, but their friendship ended when Aron moved to the Right, joining the Gaullist RPF in 1947 and contributing to the conservative newspaper *Le Figaro*. He went on to become a respected sociologist and liberal-conservative commentator on current affairs. His most famous work, *L'Opium des intellectuels* (*The Opium of the Intellectuals*, 1955), is a critique of the Marxist sympathies of French intellectuals. He and Sartre met again briefly in June 1979 when both were active in the campaign for the Vietnamese boat people.

He was audacious, I'd even go so far as to say he had a cheek which marked him out even more from the rest of us who were just kids compared to him.'[39]

Sartre's programme of studies comprised psychology, the history of philosophy, general philosophy and logic, moral philosophy and sociology, and involved reading some 300 books a year. He rarely bothered to attend lectures, preferring to work on his own from 9 a.m. to 1 p.m., then again from 4 or 5 p.m. until 8 or 9 in the evening – a working timetable that he was to observe for the rest of his life. In September 1926 Nizan left Paris for Aden, not returning until April 1927, and it was Aron who now became Sartre's chief intellectual interlocutor. Aron later recalled that Sartre 'had a new theory every week, every month. He would present it to me and I would discuss it. It was he who developed ideas and I who discussed them.'[40]

While Sartre did not affect any attitude of superiority towards those he respected or considered his friends, he treated others with contempt, especially if they were religious or displayed bourgeois characteristics. The scruffy, dirty Sartre delighted in throwing water bombs at any students who returned to the École

A portrait of the nineteen-year-old Sartre at his graduation from the École normale supérieure. 1924

at night wearing formal dinner dress, and he and other non-religious students inflicted the same treatment on the École's Catholic faithful.

But Sartre's revolt was not directed only at his peers. Each year the students traditionally presented a light-hearted satirical review and in 1925 and 1926 Sartre had appeared impersonating Gustave Lanson, the head of the École and author of a famous textbook on the teaching of French in secondary school. In 1927 Sartre again impersonated Lanson in a review that was so bitingly anti-authoritarian it has been described as 'the nastiest, most violent, most scandalous ever'.[41] Sartre also attacked the 'militarization' of the École after a law had just been passed reinforcing its links with the army. The adverse publicity generated by another stunt organized by Sartre – which involved a student impersonating the aviator Charles Lindbergh (1902–74) who had recently landed in Paris after flying solo across the Atlantic Ocean – proved too much for Lanson. He resigned.

In 1928 Sartre was one of about 70 students who signed a letter protesting at the suspension from the Order of the Légion d'honneur of the historian Georges Demartial for having argued that the French government had provoked Germany into war in 1914. Sartre was also associated with a petition protesting at the requirement of students at the École to follow a two-year programme of military training. The right-wing press called it an 'odious document' and proof that the École had been taken over by revolutionaries. Sartre responded by publishing a spoof petition in the newspapers purporting to represent those students at the École who wished to demonstrate their patriotism. 'Traditions as natural as the wearing of uniforms or military training are about to be abandoned,' it warned, 'or were in danger of being so.'[42]

Besides being regarded as a brilliant student, by 1928 Sartre had established something of a reputation as a disrespectful, subversive anti-authoritarian, anti-religious, anti-bourgeois, anti-militarist. However, unlike his two closest friends, Nizan and Aron, he still showed little interest in formal left-wing politics. He was an anti-authoritarian and anti-bourgeois rebel, albeit at this stage, a rebel without a cause.

The implantation of Marxism in France was a long and uneven process and it was not until the 1880s that the ideas of the German revolutionary Karl Marx (1818–83) began to penetrate French political culture to compete with indigenous socialist and radical traditions. Sartre first read Marx in his third and fourth years at the École, but later admitted that he did not yet see its relevance to his own times.

In 1920 the Section Française de l'Internationale Ouvrière (The French Section of the [Second] Workers' International) or SFIO had split over what attitude it should adopt towards the Third International, founded by Lenin (1870–1924) in 1919. The majority left to form the Parti communiste français (French Communist Party) or PCF, taking the newspaper *L'Humanité* with them. Aron joined the student section of the SFIO in the mid-1920s, while Nizan joined the PCF. Sartre refused to get involved and even found their commitment amusing. *At the same time, I admired them because I wasn't able to engage in discussions with them . . . But it didn't interest me. For example, socialism, which had attracted many of my friends at the École normale, didn't affect me at all.*[43] Indeed, although Sartre was broadly sympathetic to Communist ideas at this time,[43] he resented Nizan's political involvement. *I hated the fact that he had got involved in politics, because I didn't feel the need to do so.*[44]

In 1925 Sartre had his first serious love affair. Simone-Camille Sans, also known as Simone Jollivet, was a beautiful woman with a reputation for sexual intrigue who frequented high-class brothels. They met at the funeral of a mutual cousin at Thiviers and stayed together for four days before their families intervened. Sartre liked to think he was rescuing Camille from a life of provincial mediocrity and spent much time and effort encouraging her to think

Born in Paris into a respectable upper-middle-class family, Simone de Beauvoir (1908–86) defied her parents by choosing to become a philosophy teacher. Nicknamed 'le Castor' ('the Beaver'), she remained very close to Sartre until his death. Her first book, *L'Invitée* (*She Came to Stay*), was published in 1943, but she is best known for her study on the role of women, *Le Deuxième Sexe* (*The Second Sex*, 1949); her novel *Les Mandarins* (*The Mandarins*, 1954), which won the Prix Goncourt; and her four-volume memoirs. In later life, Beauvoir dropped the 'de' from her name as too bourgeois. She was active in the French feminist movement from the 1970s until her death.

for herself and recommending books for her to read. For the next two years he would see her in Toulouse, where she lived with her parents, but these visits were restricted by the cost of travelling.

In 1927 Camille spent a fortnight in Paris with Sartre and turned many a head at the École ball they attended. He had to borrow money to entertain her in the style that she expected, but she was disappointed by the poor quality of the hotel he had chosen, as well as the restaurants and dance halls they frequented. Sartre wanted her to stay, but Camille returned to Toulouse and by the summer their passionate affair had ended.

In 1928 Sartre sat the *agrégation*, the final-year competitive exam at the École. To the astonishment of students and teachers alike, he failed, apparently for trying to be too original. The following year he re-sat the written exam and while revising for the oral examination he met the woman who was to be his privileged companion for the rest of his life: Simone de Beauvoir.

Beauvoir later recalled Sartre's reputation 'as a womanizer, a drunk and a bad man', and her first impression was that he was 'the dirtiest, worst dressed and also, I think, ugliest' of all the students. But when she got to know him better it was a different story. 'I saw someone who was extremely kind with everyone, very generous, who would spend ages explaining things and never getting anything back in return, and who was very amusing, very funny and who sang all sorts of songs by Offenbach and others.'[46]

When he took the *agrégation* a second time, Sartre gave the examiners what they wanted and was placed first – the 21-year-old Beauvoir coming second. (Nizan came fifth.) When Beauvoir and Sartre left each other for the summer, she was more than ever convinced that he was the man for her. As for Sartre, he had met his intellectual equal whom he would later describe as a beautiful person with *the intelligence of a man . . . and the sensitivity of a woman. That is to say I found in her exactly everything I could desire*.[47]

His old friends were somewhat displaced by Beauvoir's arrival on the scene. 'I think our relations changed when he met de Beauvoir,' said Aron. 'There had been a time when he was pleased to have me as an interlocutor. Then there was this encounter and suddenly I no longer interested him as an interlocutor. Sartre is somebody who likes to have his special interlocutor.'[48] Soon after they met, Sartre told Beauvoir that he was going to take her under his wing. He proposed a two-year agreement based on loyalty but not fidelity – or, as he expressed it, theirs would be a necessary love, but they could also pursue contingent affairs.

In November 1929 Sartre embarked on 18 months of military service. Aron arranged for him to join his company at the meteorological centre at Saint-Cyr where he was sergeant-instructor. In January 1930 Sartre was transferred to Saint-Symphorien, near Tours, where a relaxed regime left him plenty of time for reading and writing. He completed the first two sections of '*La Légende de la vérité* ('*The Legend of Truth*'). Sartre sent it to publishers, but it was rejected, though extracts subsequently appeared in *Bifur*, a review with which Nizan was closely associated.[49] Nizan had just published *Aden Arabie (Aden Arabia)*, his romanticized account of his trip to Aden. It was also a rejection of Western civilization and a quest for personal salvation.

Sartre was able to spend a lot of time with Beauvoir at Saint-Symphorien. In August she took a room in a little hotel on the Loire and spent most days with Sartre, who would pop back to the meteorological station every two hours to take a reading. They were able to indulge themselves a little, thanks to a legacy from Louise, his maternal grandmother, who had recently died. After her return to Paris, Beauvoir would visit Sartre every Sunday, and the week's leave per month enjoyed by the soldiers allowed him to spend time in Paris with Beauvoir as well as Nizan and his wife Henriette. Despite this rather relaxed lifestyle, Sartre was very depressed and his relations with Aron also deteriorated.

Sartre applied for a teaching post in Japan, but was turned down. Nizan was now teaching in Bourg-en-Bresse and in March 1931 Sartre took up a post at the *lycée* in Le Havre. Meanwhile, Beauvoir had been offered a position in Marseille, about 600 miles away. They briefly considered marrying, since married teachers were more likely to be given posts in the same town, but decided that marriage and parenthood (neither of them wanted children) would be an unacceptable constraint on their personal freedom. It was an extremely radical stance for the times.

Becoming a teacher in a French state school was problematic for the anti-authoritarian, anti-establishment Sartre. On the one hand there were clear advantages: as a state employee he would enjoy security of tenure, a regular and reasonably good salary and, importantly, have plenty of time to write. On the other hand, a teacher was a bearer of bourgeois values, a symbol of authority and power, obliged to operate within a hierarchical structure. *I remember my first day of teaching . . . saying to myself 'I'm a teacher' and it was a very disagreeable sensation. And the reason I felt that way was precisely because there was a whole realm of discipline and order that was considered to be part of teaching that was anathema to me.*[50]

In the *lycée*, although he dressed in a three-piece suit and wore a tie, Sartre was far more easy-going than his colleagues and less conventional in his behaviour. For example, at the prize-giving ceremony in July, Sartre was called upon to give a speech (as tradition demanded of the youngest teacher). Both the subject, 'Cinema as Art', and Sartre's colloquial style shocked the good burghers of Le Havre who were in the audience.

Sartre turned down lodgings in the 'respectable' part of town, opting instead for a rather seedy room in the equally seedy Hotel Printania between the station and the port. The constant comings and goings of boats, trains and hotel guests – many of whom were commercial travellers or people who had arrived on the late-night trains – was the very antithesis of the stable, mannered routine of the bourgeois milieu he was consciously rejecting. *I hear everything that people get up to during the night. The whole road goes through my room and flows over me.*[51]

Sartre and Beauvoir also travelled extensively, which was for Sartre another way of escaping from his role as a teacher. In the two years following his arrival at Le Havre they visited Spain (summer 1931), Brittany (Easter 1932), the Balearics and Spanish Morocco (summer 1932) and England (Easter 1933). And yet he still showed little interest in political developments either in France or abroad. For example, he was not much interested in the Sino-Japanese War (1937–45) that was raging in the Far East; nor in Mahatma Gandhi (1869–1948) 's campaign for independence in India. Even closer to home, he was not unduly bothered by the rise of the Nazi Party in Germany, believing, like many, that the German working class would never allow it to triumph. Holidaying in Italy in the summer of 1933, he and Beauvoir were quite happy to take advantage of the 70 per cent fare reduction on

Italian railways offered by the dictator Benito Mussolini (1883–1945) to all foreigners who visited the Fascist Exhibition.

Sartre may have loathed the bourgeoisie and 'capitalist society', but he also needed the status quo: to observe it, to denounce it, to hate it and throw bombs at it – the bombs being his writing. He was broadly sympathetic to the 'socialist experiment' being conducted in the Soviet Union, but ultimately it left him cold and he had no wish whatsoever to live under a socialist regime. For Sartre the main contradiction was not between classes, as it was for Marxists, but between the individual (especially the writer or artist) and society. Sartre did not object to the bourgeoisie primarily because it owned the means of production and exploited the workers, but because it was a smug elite with

Smoking a pipe, Sartre sits quietly in the background among a company of actors at the Café de Flore. 1943

an oppressive and repressive morality. However, he had sympathy for the working class, whom he idealized as being 'free of any bourgeois blemish'.[52] The crude simplicity of their needs and their constant struggle against the odds meant that they faced the human situation in its true colours, he argued, although he had no contact with them.

Beauvoir asserts that Sartre had considered joining the PCF but that his ideas, aims and temperament all militated against such a step. Certainly his anti-authoritarianism would have sat very uneasily with the democratic centralism of the PCF, which since 1927–8 had taken a particularly dogmatic sectarian line. Ultimately Sartre concluded that if you were a worker you had to be a Communist, and although he was sympathetic to the struggle of the proletariat, in the final analysis it was not his struggle, which lay elsewhere. Since 1931 he had been writing what Beauvoir called his 'factum on contingency', provisionally entitled *Melancholia*, but published as *La Nausée* (*Nausea*) 1938.

Sartre's commitment to personal freedom and his mission to be a writer were paramount. Writing was his very raison d'être and to be a writer he had to be free. It was only the loners who were able to grasp living reality and then reveal it to the world. A precondition to realizing this mission, therefore, was to remain free of any organizational or political commitment. Individual freedom meant perpetual detachment.

In the autumn of 1932 Beauvoir secured a teaching post in Rouen, only an hour from Le Havre and an hour and a half from Paris, where she and Sartre went as often as possible. They were not poor, but Sartre had no real notion of money. *In a funny way, money didn't exist as far as I was concerned. I got some and then I spent it*.[53] He spent money on travelling, but rarely bought objects – not even books. If by chance he acquired a book, he gave it away as soon as he had read it. All he needed was somewhere to sleep, food, drink and tobacco. Any money left over he gave away to friends, friends of friends and Beauvoir's sister Hélène, who was trying to make a living as a painter.

In September 1932 Aron had started work at the French Institute in Berlin, while writing his thesis. Talking with Sartre and Beauvoir in a Paris café, he pointed to a drink and said that if you were a phenomenologist you could talk about it philosophically. In its broadest terms, 'phenomenology' means a descriptive philosophy of experience, and Aron told them about Edmund Husserl (1859–1938), the German phenomenologist he had been studying. His account of Husserl's bid to by-pass the traditional opposition between realism and idealism and to affirm the supremacy of reason and the reality of the visible world immediately excited Sartre – in fact, he became anxious that Husserl had stolen a march on him and his ideas of contingency. Reassured that this was not the case, Sartre wanted to know more, so he replaced Aron at the French Institute in Berlin, while Aron took his place at the *lycée* in Le Havre.

Sartre arrived in Berlin in the autumn of 1933. In January that year, the leader of the Nazi Party, Adolf Hitler (1889–1945), had become German chancellor. In February the Reichstag building had been burned out. The Nazis blamed the Communists, so the German Communist Party was swiftly banned, along with all other opposition parties. Then Hitler's Nazi Party triumphed in the May elections. Anti-Semitism was rife and the banning and burning of works by 'undesirable' authors had begun.

Sartre immersed himself in Berlin life, often in the company of the wife of a prim and passionless philosophy teacher, with whom he had an affair. They discovered together the 'high-brow theatres and cinemas, low-brow beer halls, homosexual clubs, transvestites, female wrestlers, explicit sex acts and [indulged in] loud unabashed drinking bouts'.[54] Apart from experiencing Berlin low-life, Sartre was committed to two things: studying Husserl and completing the second draft of *Melancholia*. He remained steadfastly unmoved by – even uninterested in – the political drama that was unfolding around him. Unlike Aron, Sartre wrote nothing about the rise of Nazism when he returned to France in 1934, nor was he moved to join any of the emerging anti-fascist organizations.

Sartre's preoccupations were philosophical. He agreed with Husserl's notion of intentionality of consciousness. Opposing the accepted view of the time that in order to know something we draw it into our consciousness, Husserl argued that consciousness was always consciousness of something outside itself. Consciousness was not a place, but an act or a series of acts, moving out towards objects that had their own existence, independent of consciousness. By separating consciousness from its objects, Husserl affirmed their independence and objectivity. *I was absolutely pro-Husserl on certain points*, recalled Sartre, *notably on the question of intentional consciousness. There he really revealed something to me. It was there and then* [i.e. in Berlin] *that I made that discovery.*[55]

A few years later, Sartre was to part company with Husserl over the latter's insistence that there was a transcendental ego behind consciousness.[56] Sartre denied any such transcendence, arguing that the ego was neither formally nor materially in consciousness, but was outside it, in the world. It was a being in the world like any other.

After travelling with Beauvoir in Germany, Austria, Poland and Alsace, Sartre returned to France in the autumn of 1934. *On my return I was back in the clutches of Le Havre again and resumed my life as a teacher, more bitterly than before perhaps.*[57] He now became very depressed. He was only 29, but was losing his hair and saw himself as a portly, ageing, failed writer leading *a doughy, abortive existence*[58] and was convinced that nothing new would ever happen to him.

Back in the *lycée*, his behaviour in and out of class confirmed his reputation as a maverick. His students were allowed to smoke, remove their jackets and ties and engage in discussion, in the course of which they were encouraged to reflect on their own views and challenge accepted wisdom. Sartre was always subverting the formal barriers of hierarchy and authority. His pupils remembered him as approachable and friendly, and generous with his time after class when helping them prepare for exams. These friendly relations extended well beyond the classroom: he would box with his pupils, play cards with them, go drinking with them and on at least one occasion he visited a brothel with them. However, one ex-pupil also noted a certain elitism in Sartre's nonconformity: 'The students he hung out with all had special talents or skills or advantages. He was not open to all students, just the chosen few.'[59]

Sartre's depression about his life was aggravated by his experimentation with hallucinogens – and by a passionate three-way relationship with Beauvoir and Olga Kosakiewicz. In February 1935, while working on the notion of the imaginary, Sartre agreed to be injected with mescaline by an old student friend, Daniel Lagache, then a doctor at the Saint-Anne mental hospital in Paris. Although assured that the effects of the drug would last only a few hours, Sartre was haunted by terrifying hallucinations for weeks to come. They fed into, and were fed by, his work on the imaginary, and provoked a severe depression that lasted for six months. *I was writing* L'Imaginaire *and that wasn't doing me any good at all because the imaginary has a part that I call 'certain' in which consciousness itself is conscious of what an image is. So I was all the time rummaging around in my own consciousness to see what there was, and that made my head swim, which didn't help . . . I was also taking mescaline in order to know what a hallucination was.*[60] L'Imaginaire* was the second part of a weighty manuscript that Sartre submitted to the publishing house Alcan, but only the first part, *L'Imagination (The Imagination)*, was accepted, appearing in 1936. *L'Imaginaire* was published by Gallimard in 1940.

In the spring of 1935 Sartre fell passionately in love with Olga

Kosakiewicz, one of Beauvoir's pupils at the Rouen *lycée*. The daughter of a Russian nobleman and a Frenchwoman, Olga was known as 'the little Russian'. She was a pale, stormy young woman who valued emotions above ideas. *As for Olga, my passion for her burnt away my normal impurities like the flame of a Bunsen burner*,[61] wrote Sartre. He lost count of the number of times she told him she did not love him, but this never dampened his ardour: *I was on edge, anxious. Each day I waited for the moment when I would see her again.*[62]

Beauvoir found Sartre's infatuation with Olga harder and harder to bear. She had agreed not to be the only woman in his life, but refused to accept that somebody else might be. The solution was a three-way relationship. 'Instead of being a couple, we would henceforth be a trio,' she wrote. 'We believed that human relations were to be perpetually invented and that a priori no structure was the best, none was impossible.'[63] This traumatic arrangement lasted until March 1937 and Beauvoir published a fictionalized account of it in *L'Invitée* (*She Came to Stay*).

Friends once more, Olga with de Beauvoir and Nelson Algren at Cabris. 1949

'Without formulating it to myself I resented Sartre for creating this situation,' she later admitted, 'and Olga for going along with it.'[64] In the end the relationship burned itself out and Olga left Rouen.

The final event that aggravated Sartre's depressive state was the publishing house Gallimard's rejection of his *Melancholia* manuscript in 1936. *This affected me deeply*, he wrote. *I had put all of myself into this book and I had worked on it for a long time. By rejecting it they were rejecting me and my experience.*[65]

While Sartre was reeling from the effects of taking mescaline and embroiled in his mad passion for Olga, France was becoming even more politically polarized, one feature of which was the rise of extreme right-wing extra-parliamentary organizations. In 1934 the Left's position was strengthened by the decision of the PCF, the SFIO and the Radical Party to make common cause and form a Popular Front. On 14 July 1935 this newly formed unity found expression in a Bastille Day march in Paris attended by hundreds of thousands of demonstrators. Sartre and Beauvoir went along. 'Up to a point we shared this enthusiasm,' recalled Beauvoir later, 'but we had no inclination to march, sing or shout with the others. This was our attitude at the time. Events could arouse strong emotions in us, be it anger, fear or joy, but we did not participate in them. We remained spectators.'[66]

Parliamentary elections were held in April 1936 against a background of German and Italian aggression and oppression. In March 1935 Germany had introduced conscription; in September German Jews had been banned from public life; in October Mussolini ordered the invasion of Abyssinia (Ethiopia); and in March 1936, a month before the French elections, Hitler ordered the invasion of the Rhineland. There was an electoral turn-out in France of more than 80 per cent and the forces of the Popular Front won a clear, if not overwhelming, victory. They formed a left-wing government headed by Léon Blum, (1872–1950) the leader of the SFIO, which the PCF supported, while declining to serve in it.

Sartre had refused to vote in the 1936 elections and still insisted on remaining above the political fray and jealously guarding his 'independence'. *I was completely in favour of the Popular Front*, he later recalled, *but the idea of voting to give expression to my opinion never occurred to me . . . I still retained the vestiges of individu-*

alism. I felt attracted by the crowds that were making the Popular Front,
but I had no real understanding that I was part of this and that my place
was among them. I saw myself as a loner.[67]

Sartre exhibited a similar mixture of left-wing sympathy and
inaction over the Spanish Civil War (1936–9). The war was triggered by a right-wing military revolt against the democratically
elected left-wing coalition government and, according to
Beauvoir, it dominated their lives for the next two and a half
years. Spain was the country they knew best after France and they
had many Spanish friends. 'We knew that the Spanish Civil War
posed a threat to our own future,' wrote Beauvoir. 'The left-wing
press gave it as much coverage as if it had been a French affair –
and in effect it was. At all costs another Fascist state had to be
prevented from establishing itself on our borders.'[68]

But what did Sartre actually do? True, in private he opposed
the French policy of non-intervention in support of the Spanish
republicans and the closure of the border between France and
Spain. These actions were all the more disturbing since Fascist
Italy and Nazi Germany were continuing to arm the Nationalists.
Sartre was later to claim, *I supported the Spanish Republic totally,*
absolutely. I thought of myself as an anti-fascist through and through.[69]
But he found no outlet for these sentiments. *What could I do in*
1936? Fight in Spain, with my eyes? Join the Communist Party? There
were too many nasty factors involved to do that. March? Yes, but I hated
marches. I was convinced that they accomplished nothing . . . Besides, I
looked upon Spain as somewhat isolated or special, a drama, a tragedy,
but not quite part of us all, I mean, that somehow we in France, in
Europe, and therefore somehow in Spain too, we'd all come out of it.[70]

Sartre could have chosen to campaign for the Republican cause
or denounce Fascism in his writing, but such overtly political
subject matter fell outside his self-definition of a writer at the
time. Or he could have become involved, like Nizan or his
Trotskyist friend Colette Audry (1906–90) in one of the myriad

pro-Republican support committees active in France – but Sartre was determined to remain a loner.

In July 1937 the *Nouvelle Revue française* (NRF), France's most prestigious inter-war literary review, published a short story by Sartre entitled 'Le Mur'[71] ('The Wall'). Although set in Spain during the civil war, it is a story about the absurdity of death rather than the politics of the war or the need to combat Fascism. In 1938 two more short stories by Sartre appeared: 'La Chambre'[72] ('The Room') and 'Intimité'[73] ('Intimacy').

In October 1936, a few months after the Popular Front victory in France, Sartre took up a new teaching post at Laon, 150 kilometres north-east of Paris. Beauvoir began teaching at the Lycée Molière in Paris and was living in the Hotel Royal Bretagne in the rue de la Gaité. Olga, who had run away from her parents, reappeared and took a room at the same hotel. She resumed her relationship with Sartre, but soon became involved with Jacques-Laurent Bost (1916–90), one of Sartre's ex-pupils from Le Havre, whom she subsequently married. Sartre became good friends with Olga's sister Wanda, but the relationship remained platonic for the time being.

By now Beauvoir and Sartre no longer had much of a sexual relationship. In 1948, writing in broken English to her lover the American novelist Nelson Algren (1909–81), Beauvoir explained that with Sartre 'it was rather deep friendship than love; love was not very successful. Chiefly because he does not care much for sexual life. He is a warm, lively man everywhere, but not in bed. I soon felt it, though I had no experience; and little by little, it seemed useless, and even indecent, to go on being lovers. We dropped it after about eight or ten years rather unsuccessful in this way.'[74] Sartre had little interest in sex. He liked flirting, he loved the chase, the seduction, the intrigue, but the sexual act itself left him cold.

In April *Melancholia* was published as *La Nausée* (*Nausea*) at the insistence of Sartre's editor Gaston Gallimard, and in the autumn

Sartre was appointed to teach at the Lycée Pasteur in the well-heeled Paris suburb of Neuilly. He and Beauvoir took rooms in the Hotel Mistral in the rue Cels in Paris, Sartre on the third floor, Beauvoir on the second.

He had begun *Nausea* during his military service and continued working on it at Le Havre and in Berlin. Set in Bouville (Mudtown), which is largely based on Le Havre, *Nausea* tells the tale, in the form of a diary, of Antoine Roquentin as he grapples to understand the nature of existence. At its core is the notion of contingency that Sartre had been developing since his student days; and indeed, the conclusion of Roquentin's tortuous quest to understand the nature of existence is the discovery that *things are entirely as they appear to be – and* behind *them . . . there is nothing.*[75] He finally discovers the meaning of existence: *The essential thing is contingency. I mean that, by definition, existence is not necessity. To exist is simply to be there. What exists appears, lets itself be encountered, but you can never deduce it. Everything just is, this park, this town, me. When you realize this, it turns your heart upside down and everything is unstable.*[76] Moreover, everything that exists, exists in the present alone; indeed it constitutes the present. *The true nature of the present revealed itself; it was that which exists, and all that was not present did not exist. The past did not exist. Not at all. Neither in things nor even in my thoughts.*[77]

If the present is the whole of reality, the past and the future do not exist. Furthermore, if things – and people – are contingent, if they 'just are' then we are totally free and it is through our decisions and choices that we constitute ourselves. In *Nausea* Sartre also gives numerous examples of bad faith: the excuses people use to avoid accepting the contingent nature of existence. Members of the bourgeoisie, for instance, who believe their social standing or their skills bestow upon them a 'right' to exist; then there are others who attach importance to the banality of life and attempt to flee their freedom through the repetition of empty gestures and rituals; others live in the past and identify themselves with the people they were or believed themselves to be or were presented as being; others live according to the expectations of others; and some claim to find the 'meaning' of life in a political, moral or ideological system.

Nausea was on the whole well received by the critics and the success of Sartre the novelist served to enhance the reputation he had started to enjoy as a writer of short stories and philosophical texts, mostly on perception. In 1939 he published a short text on emotions,[78] an article on Husserl written during his stay in Berlin,[79] and *Le Mur* (*The Wall*) a collection of short stories comprising 'The Wall' and 'The Room' and three other hitherto unpublished tales.[80] Sartre described the theme of the collection thus: *Nobody wants to look Existence in the face. Here are five little failures – tragic or comic – and with them five lives . . . All these attempts to escape were blocked by a Wall. To flee Existence was still to exist. Existence is a plenum that people cannot leave.*[81]

The Wall earned Sartre a reputation for being an obscene writer, although this did not prevent it being nominated 'Book of the Month' in April 1939, and winning the *Roman Populiste* prize for April 1940. From 1938 Sartre had also published articles in the NRF on the American novelists William Faulkner (1897–1962)[82] and John Dos Passos (1896–1970),[83] whom he greatly admired; an attack on *La Fin de la nuit* (*The End of the Night,* 1935) by the French Catholic novelist François Mauriac (1885–1970);[84] and a book review of Nizan's *La Conspiration*[85] (*The Conspiracy*); as well as other book reviews in the literary journal *Europe*, whose editor offered Sartre a regular column. The outbreak of war in September 1939 would prevent him from accepting this.[86]

Just when Sartre was beginning to establish himself in the Parisian world of letters, the world of politics from which he had tried so assiduously to keep himself aloof started to threaten his independence. The Popular Front government, subjected to ever more hysterical attacks from the Right and the extreme Right and simultaneously criticized by the Left for being too moderate, was crumbling. It was replaced in April 1938 by a mainly Radical administration headed by Edouard Daladier (1884–1970).

By now Hitler was eyeing-up Czechoslovakia and in September he called for self-determination for the predominantly German-speaking area of the Sudetenland within its borders. It was against this background that the British Prime Minister Neville Chamberlain (1869–1940) and Daladier met Hitler and Mussolini in Munich where, on 30 September, they signed the Munich Agreement allowing Germany to occupy the Sudetenland, in the naive belief that acceding to Hitler's demands would halt any further German expansion.

After Munich I felt relieved like everybody else, recalled Sartre, *without realizing that it was a relief that implied a policy of perpetually agreeing to what Hitler did. Relief was an attitude that had to be rejected. I didn't retain it for long. I maintained it in contradiction with myself. I was against Munich in some ways but relieved that Munich had happened.* War withdrew for a while. Relieved Sartre may have been, but it was Munich that made him realize that war would break out sooner or later. *I was never convinced that war was inevitable until Munich; when everyone thought peace was at hand, I was sure war would come, one day or another.*[87]

From the beginning of 1939 the international political situation deteriorated rapidly. In January Barcelona fell to the Nationalists; in March Hitler invaded Czechoslovakia; in April Italy invaded Albania and the following month it formally concluded an alliance with Germany. In August came the thunderbolt of the signing of the non-aggression pact between Germany and the Soviet Union, until then the most vociferous opponent of Nazi Germany and Fascism. The following week Germany invaded Poland. On 2 September Sartre was called up as part of the general mobilization and on 3 September Britain and France declared war on Germany.

The War Really Divided My Life in Two[88a]

Sartre still hoped against hope that war was not inevitable, and in a letter written at the end of August he set out a number of rational reasons why there would *not* be a war.[88] He did not, however, rule out irrationality, and a letter dated 2 September describing his call-up opens with the phrase: *Bloody stupidity* [*la connerie*] *has triumphed!*[89]

Call-up was a severe shock for Sartre, plucking him out of his comfortable niche, dragging him away from his companions and thrusting him into a world of uniforms, rules and regulations. It shattered his aspirations to individuality and independence.

He was assigned to the meteorological section of an artillery unit that moved around from small town to small town to the east and north of Strasbourg, not far from the front line. Despite the trauma of being called up, Sartre had a pretty easy time of it for the nine months of the so-called *drôle de guerre* or Phoney War before hostilities began. He did not mix well with his fellow soldiers, but his duties were far from onerous and he spent his free time reading and writing. He wrote daily to his mother and to Beauvoir and was in regular communication with a host of other correspondents. He was writing *L'Age de raison* (*The Age of Reason*), the first volume of what became the *Roads to Freedom* trilogy, and also filled 14 notebooks, six of which were published posthumously as *Carnets de la drôle de guerre* (*War Diaries*);[90] the other eight were lost. In all, it has been estimated that Sartre wrote more than a million words at this time.

The period of the Phoney War also gave Sartre the opportunity to reflect on his previous life. He decided to abandon his individualistic detachment from what he now called his 'situation' and to engage with it instead. He and his companions had been thrown into a situation not of their choosing and this led him to redefine himself as a social being: *I was quite comfortably installed in my situation as an individualist, anti-bourgeois writer. What blew all that apart was one day in September 1939 I received my call-up papers, and had to go to the barracks at Nancy to meet fellows I didn't know who'd been called up like me. That's what introduced the social dimension into my mind. Suddenly, I understood I was a social being . . . Up until then I'd believed myself sovereign. I had to encounter the negation of my own freedom through call-up in order to become aware of the weight of the world, and of my links with all those other fellows and their links with me.*[91]

Sartre also began to see himself as a part of the broader historical and political world in which he lived. *I began to reflect upon what it meant to be historical, to be part of history that was continually being decided by collective occurrences. That made me become aware of what history meant to each of us. Each one of us was history . . . The fact is that from 1939 I no longer belonged to myself. Up until then I had believed that I was leading the life of a totally free individual. I would choose my own clothes, choose what I ate, wrote things. In my opinion I was therefore a free man within society. I didn't see at all that this life was entirely conditioned by Hitler and his armies that threatened us.*[92]

In his *War Diaries* Sartre took this line of thought a stage further: if we are a part of history, whether we like it or not, we should embrace our situation and in so doing become what he now termed authentic: *To be authentic is to realize fully one's being-in-situation, whatever that situation may happen to be . . . This presupposes a patient study of what the situation requires, and then a way of throwing oneself into it and determining oneself to 'be-for' this situation. Of course situations are not catalogued once and for all. On the contrary, they are new each time.*[93] Sartre was not abandoning his cherished notion of freedom but refining it. We are still free to choose and this choice, once made, is neither fixed nor permanent; a change in the situation may result in new choices. But it is a choice that involves engaging with one's situation. *Genuine authenticity does not consist in overflowing one's life in every direction, or in stepping back to judge it, or in perpetually freeing oneself from it, but on the contrary in plunging into it and becoming an integral part of it.*[94]

Sartre contrasted his belief that freedom should be rooted in the situation with the individualistic freedom he had espoused before the war. *So there I am, 'up in the air', with no ties . . . The death of my father, my mother's remarriage and my disagreements with my step-father released me at an early age from any family influence. The hostility of my schoolfellows at La Rochelle taught me to fall back on my own resources . . . I feel no solidarity with anything, not even with myself. I don't need anybody or anything. Such is the character I have made for myself in the course of the 34 years of my life . . . I have no liking for this character, and I want to change. What I have realized is that freedom is not the Stoic detachment from loves and goods at all. On the contrary, it supposes a deep rootedness in the world.*[95]

Sartre's own situation changed dramatically as the German army advanced into France and Belgium. On 23 May 1940 his friend Paul Nizan was killed near Dunkirk and on 21 June, Sartre's birthday, Sartre was taken prisoner and subsequently transferred to a prisoner-of-war camp in Trier (Trèves). Sartre and history had collided with a vengeance. His experience as a POW only served to reinforce his new perception of himself as a social being. *I rediscovered in the Stalag a form of collective existence I hadn't know since the École normale and I can say that in the final analysis I was happy . . . What I liked about the camp was being part of a large group.*[96]

In his semi-autobiographical account of life in the camp[97] he explains how it was impossible for the individual to remain outside camp 'society'. Private life did not exist; a basic level of hygiene had to be maintained to prevent the spread of disease;

Sartre in uniform during the time of his military conscription

each man's actions had an impact on his fellows. This mutual dependency was a general feature of the POW camps: 'The courage of some, the defeatism of others influenced the outlook of the camp inmates in general. The individual no longer acted anonymously or in isolation; his decisions were felt and registered by the group whose fortunes he shared.'[98]

Sartre may have enjoyed being part of the crowd but this did not stop vestiges of his old elitism surfacing as he gravitated towards a group of priests *who in a bourgeois sense of the term represented an elite . . . and at the same time – another example of elitism – I was first assigned to the infirmary just because some guy there asked for me, and where I did nothing (elitism) and later I was assigned to the barracks for artists and performers whose job it was to entertain the prisoners on Sundays. That too was a kind of elitism.*[99] It was as a member of the 'artistic elite' that Sartre wrote and acted in a play, *Bariona ou le fils de tonnerre* (*Bariona or the Son of Thunder*), which was performed in front of the prisoners during Christmas 1940.

Sartre's play clearly illustrates his desire to identify with the mass of the prisoners. *For me, the important aspect of this experience was that as a prisoner I was going to be able to address my fellow prisoners and talk about the problems that we shared.*[100] Set in Palestine during the Roman occupation, *Bariona*,[101] according to Sartre, carried a message of hope and a call to resistance. Although the Germans seemed to be oblivious to the play's message, he was convinced that *the French prisoners understood everything and my play interested them.*[102] However, one of his priest friends, Abbé Perrin, thought it was only the intellectuals in the camp who understood the play in the context of Sartre's ideas on freedom and responsibility. The majority took it to be a Christian play, albeit with a contemporary edge.[103]

Early in 1941 Sartre was released from the camp thanks to false medical papers which declared he was a semi-blind civilian. By early April he was back in Paris, which was now occupied by the

Germans. The German army had reached the capital on 14 June, by which time the French government had decamped to Bordeaux where Marshal Philippe Pétain (1856–1951), replacing Paul Reynaud as head of government, immediately sought an armistice. France was divided into four zones: the 'forbidden zone' (the Nord and Pas-de-Calais regions), Alsace-Lorraine (which reverted to Germany), the Occupied Zone (northern and south-western France including Paris and the Channel and Atlantic coastlines) and the Unoccupied Zone (the southern part of the country under the jurisdiction of the French government, which soon established itself in the spa town of Vichy). Later that year Pétain would appeal to his countrymen to collaborate 'in honour and dignity' with their German occupiers. In contrast, on 18 June 1940 an obscure Brigadier-General Charles de Gaulle, who had left Bordeaux for London, made a BBC broadcast calling for French resistance. So obscure was he, at the time, that the BBC did not keep a recording of the broadcast.

Meanwhile, Sartre decided to assume his 'historicity' and act upon his situation. *That's what seemed to be the first thing to do on coming back to Paris, to create a resistance group. To try, step by step, to win over the majority of the people to the Resistance and so bring into being a violent movement that would drive out the Germans.*[104] To this end he gathered his 'family' round him: Beauvoir and Olga and her sister Wanda, plus Jacques-Laurent Bost, Olga's husband, and Jean Pouillon, like Bost, an ex-pupil from Le Havre. They soon linked up with Maurice Merleau-Ponty (1907–61), a former student of the École normale who knew Beauvoir and had formed an embryonic resistance group called Sous la Botte (Under the Jackboot) with some students from the École.

One of the first tasks was to give this new grouping a name and Sartre's proposal Socialisme et Liberté (Socialism and Freedom) was accepted. It shows just how far Sartre's ideas had moved. *At that point* [1941] *I had become a Socialist. I had become one partly because on the one hand our prisoner's life was to put it briefly, a kind of socialism – a dismal kind but it was a collective life, a community.*[105] As for freedom, this had been fundamental to Sartre's pre-war thinking and was central to the philosophical treatise he had begun during the Phoney War and which would be published in 1943 as *L'Être et le néant* (*Being and Nothingness*). Furthermore, freedom was the very antithesis of Nazism. Sartre made clear the synthesis of Socialism and Freedom by arguing that its two purposes were *to fight for our freedom now and to do so in the hope of establishing a new collective society in which we would all be free because no one would have the power to exploit anyone else.*[106]

This tiny resistance group – comprising socialists, anarchists, Marxists and anti-Marxists – spent the next few months discussing, writing and distributing a bulletin and putting up posters. By June Socialism and Freedom had about 50 members divided into cells of five members each. Their inexperience was only too apparent: one member was caught distributing the bulletin, but escaped with a few months in prison thanks to a lenient magistrate; another left a briefcase in the Metro containing copies of the bulletin and a text of a future editorial. Sartre believed that the group had to prepare for a post-Nazi future and duly produced a hundred-page blueprint covering all aspects of the future state, but no copies of this document have survived.

In the summer of 1941 Sartre and Beauvoir crossed over into the Unoccupied Zone and travelled south to try to enlist other intellectuals. In Grasse they met the novelist André Gide, who offered no help and left France for Tunisia a few months later. Sartre also visited André Malraux (1901-76) who had been a fellow-traveller and had fought in Spain. Malraux, disillusioned by the outcome of the Spanish Civil War and the German-Soviet pact and now living in luxury on the French Riviera told Sartre he didn't think resistance was possible and that he was relying on Russian tanks and American planes to win the war. In Marseille

Sartre met Daniel Mayer (1909–96), who had replaced Léon Blum (who was now in prison) as the head of the SFIO. In response to Sartre's request for suggestions as to what specific tasks the Socialism and Freedom group might undertake, Mayer suggested they could send a birthday card to Blum.

Sartre and Andre Gide in the garden of Gide's house in Cabris. 1950

Sartre and Beauvoir returned to Paris dejected and demoralized. Following the invasion of the Soviet Union by Germany in June, the PCF had thrown itself into the Resistance, and Gaullist resistance networks were also beginning to establish themselves. There was little political space for an amateurish outfit like Socialism and Liberty and in October the decision was taken to disband. That same month Sartre took up a teaching post at the Lycée Condorcet in Paris.

Sartre should be given credit for attempting to 'do something' at a time when there was virtually no organized resistance at all. The people involved in Socialism and Liberty were only too aware of the risks. The members of another tiny resistance group based at the Musée de l'homme (Museum of Mankind) had been arrested in March 1941 and tortured before being shot in January 1942. Sartre showed considerable bravery, optimism and determination. On the other hand, he had little aptitude for the project he had undertaken. Contemporaries refer to him at this time as 'absolutely not cut out for this sort of clandestine work';[107a] 'a political illiterate, totally unable to decipher the papers of his time'[107] and even 'a buffoon';[108] 'someone who had got lost in the quicksands of action, having neither the background, the skills nor the means to realize the clandestine project he had devised'.[109] Or as the playwright Samuel Beckett (1906–89) put it: 'There were always those whom no one took seriously, neither the resisters nor the Gestapo. Sartre seemed to many people to be among those'.[110]

Some of Socialism and Freedom's members joined the PCF, but this was not an option for Sartre. The Communists disliked his writings and mistrusted him because of his friendship with Nizan, who had resigned from the Party when it supported the German-Soviet pact and was still, even after his death, considered a traitor.

The Communists had also spread a rumour that Sartre had been released from the POW camp to spy on the Resistance.

In Paris Beauvoir and Sartre spent much of their time in the Café de Flore where Sartre finished a new play *Les Mouches* (*The Flies*), which he had started in the summer of 1941. He also began *Le Sursis* (*The Reprieve*), the second part of the *Roads to Freedom* trilogy, and was busy writing *Being and Nothingness*.

Sartre and de Beauvoir at a Café. 1946

During the Occupation the Nazis wanted to give the impression that it was 'business as usual' and the capital's artistic and literary life was thriving. The *Nouvelle Revue française* had suspended publication, but was revived under the editorship of the pro-Nazi novelist Pierre Drieu la Rochelle (1893–1945) and a plethora of other publications made their appearance – all subject, of course, to Nazi censorship. Most resistance writers refused to work for the collaborationist press, but in June 1941 Sartre was offered a weekly column in *Comœdia*. It also published his lengthy review of *Moby Dick* by Herman Melville (1819–91), which had only recently appeared in French translation.

Comœdia's editor had assured Sartre that the journal was not subject to German censorship because it dealt with cultural rather than political affairs. This was either naive or disingenuous, for *Comœdia*'s devotion to German and European culture formed a bridge between Occupied France and Nazi Germany and provided a 'soft' way of promoting National Socialist ideas. Sartre soon realized this and declined to continue with his weekly column, but he did make two more appearances in the magazine: in April 1943 he was interviewed about *The Flies*[111] and in February 1944 he contributed an article in honour of the playwright Jean Giraudoux, who had just died.[112]

In October 1942, following the Allied landings in North Africa, the Nazis occupied all of France, thus undermining any pretensions to autonomy by the Vichy government. The tide of the war was now turning against the Axis forces and the French Resistance was growing in strength and effectiveness. During the winter of 1942–3 Sartre was approached by Claude Morgan, a leading PCF intellectual, and asked to join the Comité national des écrivains (National Writers' Committee) and contribute to *Les Lettres françaises*, a clandestine cultural and literary Resistance publication of which Morgan was editor. At Sartre's request, Morgan put a stop to the malicious rumours about Sartre being a spy and later enthusiastically recalled Sartre's contributions to the journal and his constructive role at CNE meetings, where he always strove to establish unity.

Sartre contributed four articles to *Les Lettres françaises*, the first of which was an attack on Pierre Drieu la Rochelle.[114] In his second article Sartre argued that 'collaborationist literature' was a contradiction in terms, since literature is an act of communication that demands the freedom of the reader.[116] His third article attacked a play by Marcel Aymé (1902–67) which had been praised by collaborationist critics;[118] and in his fourth contribution Sartre set out views on post-Liberation cinema.[120] Sartre also contributed articles to *Cahiers du Sud*, another resistance publication.

After seeing his play *Bariona* performed in the POW camp, Sartre had written to Beauvoir: *I want you to know that I've certainly got a gift as a playwright . . . and I'll take up theatre later.*[121] In the summer of 1941, travelling through the Unoccupied Zone with

her, Sartre had begun work on *The Flies*. Taking as its theme the notions of freedom and responsibility, it was completed in 1942, but for financial reasons was not staged until the following year, when it opened at Le Théatre de la Cité on 3 June. It was at the dress rehearsal of the play that Sartre first met Albert Camus, although each was familiar with and had reviewed the other's works.[122]

In order to get *The Flies* past the German censors, Sartre turned to Greek mythology. He reworked the myth of Orestes,

Albert Camus

who returns to the city of Argos to avenge the murder of his father Agamemnon, killing Aegisthus and his mother Clytemnestra and assuming full responsibility for his actions. In interviews at the time Sartre emphasized the play's philosophical themes: *I wanted to deal with the tragedy of freedom as contrasted with the tragedy of fate. In other words, what my play is about could be summed up thus: 'How does a man behave faced with an act which he has committed, for which he accepts all the consequences and assumes full responsibility, even if, at the same time, he is horrified by what he has done?'*[123]

However, after the Occupation, without denying the philosophical dimensions of the play, he insisted on its political relevance. *The Flies*, he said, was a reaction against the spirit of repentance and remorse that Pétain and other collaborators had peddled, trying to convince the French that the Occupation was a punishment for their past errors and moral laxity. On the first anniversary of the armistice, for instance, Pétain had declared in a radio broadcast to the nation: ' You are suffering and you will go on suffering for a long time yet, for we have not finished expiating all our faults.'[124]

Albert Camus (1913–60) was born into an impoverished family in Algeria. He attended university in Algiers and later formed an avant-garde theatre company. He was briefly a member of the Communist Party and subsequently moved to France. During the Occupation he was involved in the Combat resistance group. He developed his doctrine of 'the absurd' through his novels *L'Étranger* (*The Outsider*, 1942) and *La Peste* (*The Plague*, 1947), a philosophical essay, *Le Mythe de Sisyphe* (*The Myth of Sisyphus*, 1942), and a play, *Caligula* (1944). After the Liberation his name was linked with Sartre's, but their friendship suffered when they took different positions during the Cold War. The final rupture occurred in 1952 following the publication of *L'Homme révolté* (*The Rebel*, 1951). Camus was awarded the Nobel Prize for Literature in 1957 and died in a car crash in 1960.

From 1941 to 1943 many people were extremely keen for the French to immerse themselves in repentance, said Sartre in 1948, *the aim was to plunge us into such a state of repentance, of shame, that we would be incapable of putting up any resistance . . . By writing my play, I was trying with the means at my disposal, however feeble they might be, to help root out some of this sickness of repentance, this subservience to repentance and shame. The French people needed to be set on their feet again, their courage needed to be restored.*[125]

In *The Flies* Aegistheus and Clytemnestra can be seen to represent Hitler and Pétain, while the 'curse' of Agamemnon is the demoralization following the Fall of France. Similarly, the alliance between Zeus and the royal couple represents the complicity between the Catholic Church and Vichy. Orestes' murder of the king and queen can be seen as an act of revolt against the Nazis and Vichy, while Electra represents those who wanted to act against Vichy and the occupying forces, but were unable to do so and take responsibility for their actions.

The Flies also addressed the moral issue of reprisals by the Nazis for attacks against members of the occupying forces. In August 1941, following the assassination of a German officer, the Nazis announced that any French person arrested would be considered a hostage and that in the event of any future attacks hostages would be shot. By the end of 1942 some 1,500 'hostages' had been executed. *At that time the Wehrmacht had started executions with six or eight hostages shot for every three Germans*, Sartre recalled in 1948, *and that had very important moral implications. Not only were these hostages innocent but, it should be emphasised, they had done nothing against the Wehrmacht, and most were not even members of the Resistance . . . The problem of these attacks was, therefore, of prime importance. Anyone who carried out an attack had to know that, unless he gave himself up, fellow Frenchmen would be shot at random. So he was subject to a second form of repentance: he had to resist the temptation to give himself up. This is how the allegory of my play is to be understood.*[126]

Sartre patiently responded to criticism that Orestes (representing the Resistance) should not have left the city of Argos alone at the end of the play: *The political circumstances of the time led me to present things in this way. Orestes personified the different strands of the Resistance who, in the absence of a detailed programme, were endeavouring first to free the French people from oppression. The programme was only drawn up after the Liberation.*[127] Or, as he remarked on another occasion: *The Resistance was only an individual solution . . . in our eyes it had above all a symbolic value.*[128]

Although *The Flies* was not a great success, Sartre claimed that *the people who did come* [to the play] *were, for the most part, young people who had a certain sense of what resistance meant, and who understood the deeper meanings of the play.*[129] However, a comprehensive analysis of the critical response to the play undertaken by Ingrid Galster concluded that most of the drama critics 'did not grasp the political message of the play as pertaining to what was happening in France at the time'.[130] As with *Bariona*, Sartre overestimated the extent to which his audience understood his political message. As Galster noted: 'Only *readers* of a *reasonably high intellectual level* were able to understand *The Flies* on a philosophical and a political plane.'[131]

In the same month as *The Flies* opened, Gallimard published Sartre's weighty philosophical tome *Being and Nothingness*, subtitled 'An Essay on Phenomenological Ontology', but it attracted little immediate attention. Nevertheless, in the words of the American scholar Ronald Aronson, it is remarkable 'for its passionate argument against all determinism and for human freedom, and its exploration of the meanings of our involvement and action in the world. At its most profound, it was a strikingly original discussion of the ways in which individuals make themselves unique: of their consciousness, their subjectivity, their roles as centres of meaning, sources of values, creators of possibilities'.[132]

Sartre begins by positing two mutually irreconcilable forms of being: *l'être en-soi* (being in-itself) and *l'être pour-soi* (being for-itself). Being in-itself is simply being. *Being is. Being is in-itself. Being is what is.*[133] Being for-itself, on the other hand, is synonymous with consciousness. It is always consciousness of something, always reaching out towards the material world beyond it, although by itself it is nothing. It is like a hole at the very heart of being. By positing the notions of being in-itself and being for-itself, Sartre believed he had found a third way between idealism, which reduced reality to humankind's comprehension of it, and materialism, which reduced consciousness to a mere product or reflection of the material world. This 'reaching out' of consciousness, this engagement with the world in a myriad of ways, prepares the ground for one of the central themes of the book: freedom.

Freedom, for Sartre, is the permanent ability of every individual to go beyond his or her present state and situation. The individual does not exist in order to be free, because there is no difference between 'being' and 'being free'. Whatever situation an individual is in, he is free to choose his course of action. Even the slave is free, in that he can choose to rebel against his bondage or to passively accept his lot. Indeed in a situation of oppression, choice weighs all the more heavily. This is the theme developed by Sartre in a text published a month after the Liberation of Paris. It begins: *We were never freer than during the German Occupation.*[134]

It is through individual choices that we create ourselves. These choices are not determined by history, fate or circumstance. Having made a choice, the individual can go on to make very different choices to respond to his circumstances – just as Sartre chose to engage with politics, having chosen to remain aloof before the war. He therefore rules out any kind of essentialism: there are no fixed 'givens', other than those imposed by what he called our 'facticity' – physical limitations, for instance. (An 80-year-old woman cannot choose to be a champion Olympic athlete, though if she is still mobile, she can choose whether or not to take regular exercise.) We exist and then, through a continuous process that lasts until death, we constitute ourselves through the choices we make. Or as Sartre put it, *existence precedes essence*.[135]

But because we are condemned to be free, we are overwhelmed by a sense of responsibility. This produces a state of anxiety and a desire to flee this freedom. We are constantly tempted to deny that we are free and try to behave as if we were simply a being in-itself. Sartre calls this refusal to accept that we are free *bad faith*. 'It is bad faith to pretend that I am not free, to act as if what is really my choice is, or could be, a condition, to *become* a role, as if I did not have to choose and recreate it at every moment – above all, to deny that I constantly escape myself, go beyond myself, project new goals.'[136] All determinism, all essentialism ('That's just the way I am' or 'If it wasn't for *x* I would . . .'), comprise examples of bad faith, because determinism and essentialism deny the fluidity and the instability of freedom, which is inescapable.

Sartre also explores our relations with the Other. The individual is not alone in a world consisting simply of beings in-themselves (or objects). The individual inhabits a world with other 'beings for-themselves'. 'Because we live in a world with others . . . we are condemned to live in a *conflict of freedoms*. The other threatens my freedom and makes me aware that the world is not my own. He steals my world away from me. He takes over my projects and gives them another meaning, his meaning. He rewrites my script.'[137]

Sartre offers three pessimistic solutions to our relations with the Other: you can make yourself into a desirable object, but this is simply an attempt to flee from freedom by placing yourself in servile unfreedom (masochism); you can try to dominate the Other (sadism); or you can attempt to be indifferent. Sartre argues that this third option is impossible and we are left with the other two unenviable options.

Ultimately, the individual is trapped both ways. First, there is the internal conflict between the being for-itself and the being in-itself. 'Man is condemned to self-division, to be what he is not and not to be what he is.'[138] Second, the being for-itself (individual) is condemned to an existence that is fundamentally irreconcilable with the existence of beings for-themselves (the Other). According to Sartre, the individual can only be authentic when he accepts his condition as a useless passion.

Being and Nothingness was published on 25 June 1943 and during his summer holiday Sartre continued to work on *The Reprieve*. On his return to Paris, however, he stopped writing his novel and began writing his third play, initially called *Les Autres (The Others)*, but renamed *Huis Clos* (translated as *In Camera* in Britain and as *No Exit* in the United States). He wrote it in two weeks and it opened in Paris on 27 May 1944. Exploring in dramatic form some of the ideas in *Being and Nothingness* concerning relations with the Other, *Huis Clos* examines the relations between two women, Inès and Estelle, and one man, Garcin, condemned to live together in hell for all eternity.

Initially, Wanda was to have been one of the actresses and Sartre invited Camus to direct the play and take the part of Garcin, but although both were involved in some early rehearsals, neither appeared in the final production. A number of critics, notably in the Catholic press, attacked the play for its pessimism, which seemed to be summed up by its most famous line: *Hell is other people*. However, Sartre rejected this interpretation. *'Hell is other people' has always been misunderstood*, he complained in 1965. *People thought that I meant by that, that our relations with the Other were always poisonous, that they were always forbidden relations. But I meant something quite different. I meant that if the relations with the Other are twisted, then the Other can only be hell . . . The Other is, fundamentally, what is most important in ourselves, in our own understanding of ourselves.*[139]

Huis Clos was banned in Britain, but was performed in private clubs under the title *Vicious Circle*. It was a great success in the

United States, however, where it received the Donaldson Prize for the best play performed in New York (1946–7).

In August 1944 Paris was liberated. Camus, who had been active in the Combat resistance group, asked Sartre to write some articles on the Paris uprising and the days that followed. The newspaper *Combat* published seven articles that appeared under Sartre's name between 28 August and 4 September,[140] though Beauvoir subsequently claimed that she wrote them.[141]

At the Liberation Sartre was regarded by many as 'the symbol, as well as the product, of the intellectual resistance'.[142] He was even awarded the Légion d'honneur, which he naturally refused. He had formed a resistance group; he had been a member of the CNE; he had written for the underground resistance press and had fooled the German censors into allowing him to present *The Flies* in the capital, a play hailed by the Communist paper *Action* as a model of 'resistance theatre', and about which similar sentiments were expressed in *Ce Soir*, another Communist publication for which Nizan had worked.[143]

Subsequently, however, Sartre's role during the Occupation has been the subject of a number of revisions. He has been accused of having settled in comfortably during the Occupation and of engaging in 'Resistance from the Café de Flore', as Aron put it. Furthermore, Sartre was accused of advancing his career under German censorship by publishing *Being and Nothingness* and writing two plays for performance. *The Flies* was even staged in a theatre that had been 'Aryanized' (the Nazis renamed the Théâtre Sarah Bernhardt the Théâtre de la Cité because Bernhardt was Jewish). In 1972 Sartre answered his critics: *I can tell you that I asked permission to put on* The Flies *from the CNE, the CNR* [The National Resistance Committee], *the Literary Committee and the Writers' Committee and they all said yes.*[144]

While Sartre may not have been quite the intellectual resistance hero he was made out to be at the Liberation, his anti-nazism and anti-Pétainism are beyond doubt. To be sure, he made compromises, but so did many others. With very few exceptions the myth of the 'pure resistance hero' is just that – a myth. The compromises he made to survive and to maintain his intellectual life should not overshadow the repugnance he felt for the Nazis, for their ideology and that of the Vichy regime. Sartre never claimed to be a resistance fighter, only a writer who resisted.

Existentialism and Communism

The immediate post-Liberation period was one of wild euphoria. 'Day and night with our friends, chatting, drinking, wandering the streets, laughing, we celebrated our deliverance,' wrote Beauvoir. 'And all those who celebrated it like us became our friends, close or not so close. What an orgy of fraternity.'[145]

In December 1944 Sartre accepted Camus's invitation to travel to the United States as a journalist for *Combat* and left France a month later. While his articles for *Combat* and *Le Figaro* revealed his enthusiasm for many aspects of the American way of life, they also highlighted the contradiction in US society between conformity and individualism, egalitarian social relations and the inequality of power, and the issue of racism. Sartre met a number of French cultural figures who had sought refuge there during the war, including the anthropologist Claude Lévi-Strauss (*b*.1908), the surrealist André Breton (1896–1966) and the painter Fernand Léger (1881–1955). In Hollywood he met Nizan's widow, Henriette, and attended a private showing of Orson Welles (1915–85)'s *Citizen Kane*, about which he wrote a critical article.[146] Sartre and other French journalists were introduced to President Franklin D Roosevelt (1882–1945) a few weeks before his death, and Sartre noted *his profoundly human charm* and *generous warmth*.[147]

It was also in the United States that Sartre met Dolorès Vanetti, a lively and vivacious French national who was responsible for preparing programmes for *The Voice of America*. She had married a rich American doctor from whom she was in the process of separating, and by the time Sartre left for Paris in May they had agreed to spend more time together.

In September Paris experienced what Beauvoir called an 'existentialist offensive', triggered by the simultaneous publication of Sartre's *The Age of Reason* and *The Reprieve*, and of her existentialist Resistance novel *Le Sang des autres* (*The Blood of Others*). A month later, Beauvoir's existentialist play *Les Bouches inutiles* (*The Useless Mouths*) opened and the first issue of the *Les Temps modernes* – a new review co-edited by Sartre and Merleau-Ponty – went on sale. Sartre's reputation as a philosopher, a novelist and a playwright was now firmly established and Sartrean existentialism, with its epicentre in Saint Germain-des-Prés on the Left Bank, was all the rage.

Sartre still frequented the Café de Flore or the nearby Les Deux Magots to write or meet friends, including the jazz trumpeter, poet and author Boris Vian (1920–59), Vian's wife Michelle, with whom Sartre began a clandestine affair in December 1945, the Swiss sculptor Alberto Giacometti (1901–66), the novelist Nathalie Sarraute (1900–99) and of course members of the 'family'. The existentialist 'fever' intensified after Sartre's lecture 'L'Existentialisme est un humanisme' ('Existentialism and Humanism') on 29 October, which was so popular that people had to be turned away and women fainted in the crush.

Existentialism was inextricably associated with Sartre and to a lesser extent Beauvoir. 'My baggage weighed little,' she wrote, 'but Sartre was hurled brutally into becoming a celebrity and my name was associated with his.'[148] As a philosophy, existentialism chimed with the France of the immediate post-war years. With freedom at its core, it appealed to those whose formal freedoms had been denied during the Occupation, and its emphasis on choice and responsibility allowed people to review their recent past, while engaging with the present and building a new future. But it was also the first media craze of the post-war period and articles on existentialism ranging from the serious to the scandalous filled the pages of the post-Liberation newspapers. Sartre and Beauvoir were followed everywhere, photographed and accosted in the street by strangers. Although Sartre had hankered after fame and recognition, he had always assumed it would come late in life, if not posthumously. *It is not pleasant to be treated as a public monument during one's lifetime*, he observed.[149]

While many people, especially young Parisians, enthusiastically embraced existentialism – or what they understood by the term – and flocked to the cafés and clubs of St Germain-des-Prés dressed typically in black, traditionalists attacked it with equal vigour, deploring what they saw as Sartre's moral depravity and his obsession with sordid situations and unsavoury characters. While the brickbats from the Right and the Catholic Church mattered little to the anti-authoritarian Sartre, who now saw himself as a man of the Left, he was upset by the attacks from the French Communist Party which, boosted by its role in the Resistance, was now attracting about a quarter of the votes in the post-war elections.

Sartre had not voted in the elections and had no intention of applying to join the Party since his socialism was at odds with the centralized, hierarchical variant offered by the PCF. *For my part, I had become a convinced socialist*, he wrote, *but an anti-hierarchical and libertarian one, one in favour of direct democracy*.[150] Nonetheless, he believed that he and the Party shared enough common ground for them to work together (as they had during the war when Sartre was a member of the CNE) and he envisaged playing the role of a critical supporter. The Party, however, had other ideas.

At the end of 1944 the Communist newspaper *Action* had given Sartre space to respond to some of the criticisms levelled against existentialism,[151] but the Party was soon subjecting Sartre to a barrage of personal, philosophical and political attacks. It denounced the links between Sartrean existentialism and the 'decadent pessimism' of the German philosopher Martin Heidegger (1889–1976), who had been a member of the Nazi Party. The Communists accused Sartre of advocating quietism (letting others do what I cannot do), and objected that his abstract, idealist notion of the Individual was devoid of any class dimension. Sartre later concluded that they had attacked him because existentialism was a threat to the Party and its orthodox Marxism. *I attribute this break* [with the PCF] *to the fact that I was starting to be well known, especially as the author of* Being and Nothingness, *which could only displease them. One of the leaders told me that I was a brake on the movement that was drawing young intellectuals towards the Party.*[152]

In January 1946 General de Gaulle, unable to gain support for his belief in the necessity of a strong executive, resigned as head of the Government. At the time Sartre was on a lecture tour of American universities, although the main reason for the trip was to be with Dolorès in New York. *She is absolutely charming and we never argue,*[153] he wrote to Beauvoir in January, adding in another letter written in February that *apart from you, she is the person I know best.*[154] In New York Sartre did little writing and enjoyed exploring the city with Dolorès (who was still technically married). They had agreed to spend two or three months together every year, but back in Paris in April Sartre reassured Beauvoir, who felt threatened by Dolorès: *She's enormously important to me, but you're the one I'm with.*[155]

In October Sartre and his mother moved into a small flat that Anne-Marie had bought after Mancy's death in January 1945 and where he stayed until 1962. *Until then I had always lived in a hotel, did my work in a café, ate in a restaurant and, this was very important for me, never owned anything.*[156] Now he had as his base the best room in the fourth-floor flat in the rue Bonaparte, overlooking the square in front of the Saint Germain-des-Prés church and a short walk from the Café de Flore and Les Deux Magots. For the first time in his life he began buying books that soon filled the shelves in his room, which doubled as bedroom and study.

In June he engaged a secretary, Jean Cau (1925–93), who was to remain in the post until 1957. Initially Cau's duties were to keep unwanted admirers at bay and to answer letters, but he was also a useful go-between and Sartre would send him letters for Michelle Vian when he was away from Paris. By now, Sartre had four important women in his life: Dolores, Wanda, Michelle and Simone de Beauvoir.

In November 1946 a double-bill of Sartre's plays opened at the Théâtre Antoine: *Morts sans sépulture* (*Men Without Shadows*) featuring Wanda (under her stage name of Marie-Olivier) and *La Putain respectueuse* (*The Respectful Prostitute*). *Men Without Shadows* is set during the Occupation and caused an outcry, mainly because of the scenes depicting the torture of members of the Resistance by French collaborators. At the first night, Aron's wife was so overcome by the torture scenes that she walked out, accompanied by her husband, which Sartre took as a personal snub.

The Respectful Prostitute was based on an incident in Alabama in 1931 when nine black men were accused of raping two white prostitutes and sentenced to death in the electric chair. It reflected Sartre's sensitivity to the racism to which American blacks were subjected, which had been heightened by his growing friendship with author Richard Wright (1908–60), whom he had met in America and whose novel *Native Son* (1940) is about a black man who murders a white woman and is sent to the electric chair. Inevitably, perhaps, Sartre found himself accused of being anti-American, a charge he vigorously refuted. He was attacking racism, not America.

In the same month as Sartre's double-bill opened, Britain's wartime leader Winston Churchill (1874–1965) spoke of an 'iron curtain' that was starting to divide Europe. As the world became polarized, Sartre's sympathies lay with the Soviet Union, but he was far from being a crypto-Communist or fellow traveller. In June 1946 the first part of 'Matérialisme et révolution' ('Materialism and Revolution') appeared,[157] in which Sartre developed his objections to the orthodox (i.e. Stalinist) interpretation of dialectical materialism (the philosophy underpinning Marxism). In the second part, published the following month,[158] he set out his own non-deterministic revolutionary philosophy built around the notion of freedom.

Sartre's sympathy with the Soviet Union led to strained relations with his former friends, notably Camus and Aron. In the autumn of 1946 Camus and Sartre spent a lot of time drinking and discussing politics with the novelist Arthur Koestler (1905–83). Koestler had been a Communist militant, but was now an implacable anti-Communist who had analysed the Moscow Show Trials in his semi-fictional *Darkness at Noon* (1940). Camus, who had joined the Communist Party in the 1930s, was

Arthur Koestler relaxing with his dog Sabby. 1949

now hostile to both the Soviet Union and the PCF and found himself in agreement with much that Koestler was saying.

At the end of October, Sartre, Camus and Koestler met the French writer André Malraux to discuss the creation of a new human rights organization since, in Koestler's view, the existing one was effectively run by the Communists. Camus supported the idea, but in the face of Malraux's scepticism and Sartre's hostility, the plan was dropped. In December, at a party hosted by the Vians, Camus accused Merleau-Ponty of justifying the Moscow Trials in his article 'The Yogi and the Proletarian', the title being a parody of Koestler's essay collection *The Yogi and the Commissar* (1945). Sartre sided with Merleau-Ponty and Camus stormed off. He and Sartre remained estranged until the following March. Aron, unlike Camus, had been on the original editorial committee of *Les Temps modernes*, but as Sartre's review consolidated itself on the Left, he began to feel politically marginalized and pointedly distanced himself from it. His last contribution appeared in June.

The year 1946 also saw the publication of Sartre's *Réflexions sur la question juive* (*Reflections on the Jewish Question*),[159] an extended version of an article he had published earlier,[160] in which he considered the notion of authenticity in relation to Jews. Aware of the responsibility of non-Jews in permitting the Holocaust to happen, Sartre supported the Jewish struggle against the British in Palestine. In February 1948 he appeared as a witness at the trial of one of his students charged with possessing arms destined for the anti-British campaign. The following month he declared it was the duty of non-Jews to support the Jews and their cause.[161] In May he announced that he was in favour of the creation of Israel, which should be an independent, free and peaceful state,[162] and in December he joined the French League for a Free Palestine, which was committed to the creation of a Jewish homeland in Palestine.

In January 1947 Beauvoir left Paris for a lecture tour of the United States, knowing that Dolorès intended coming to Paris during her absence in order to be with Sartre. Towards the end of Beauvoir's tour, Sartre asked her to delay her return because Dolores was still in Paris. In May Beauvoir began an affair with the novelist Nelson Algren which lasted until the mid-1960s. In that same year Gallimard published Sartre's biography of the nineteenth-century poet Charles Baudelaire (1821–67), originally written in 1944 as an introduction to a post-war edition of the poet's *Écrits intimes* (*Intimate Journals*, 1946), but Sartre was lambasted for having discussed only the man and ignoring his works. In his conclusion, redolent of the existentialism that guided his analysis, Sartre wrote of Baudelaire: *The free choice that the man makes for himself is absolutely identical with what people call his destiny*.[163] For Sartre, Baudelaire *is the man who chose to see himself as if he were somebody else. His life is nothing but the story of this failure.*[164]

Between February and July 1947 *Les Temps modernes* published Sartre's 'Qu'est-ce que la littérature?' ('What is Literature?').[165] Sartre expanded his much-contested advocacy of a literature of commitment, which he had outlined in his 'Présentation des *Temps modernes*' ('Introduction to *Les Temps modernes*', October 1945) and 'La Nationalisation de la littérature' ('The Nationalization of Literature',[166] November 1945). 'What is Literature?' also revealed Sartre's views on the Soviet Union and the revolutionary potential of the working class and the PCF at this time.

He rejected the PCF's view of the Soviet Union as a workers' paradise on earth where all social problems had been (or soon would be) eliminated. He remained broadly sympathetic towards the Soviet Union, but believed that the revolutionary process had stalled and, *contained within the Soviet borders, it congealed into a conservative nationalism*.[167] While the Soviet Union remained a beacon of hope for millions of workers, Sartre was reluctant to be too critical of it. To have gone further, in the polarized world of the late 1940s, would have thrust Sartre, in the eyes of the public, into the camp of the conservative, pro-capitalist cold-warriors.

This was out of the question for the anti-authoritarian socialist that Sartre now considered himself to be.

Sartre rejected the Communists' view that the working class had a historically determined emancipatory role, but he nonetheless believed that the working class was *trying to liberate itself and at the same time liberate all humanity for always from oppression*.[168] His problem, already identified in 'Materialism and Revolution', was that it was impossible for him to reach the French working class. *Unhappily, these people to whom we* must *speak are separated from us by an iron curtain in our own country*, he wrote. *The majority of the proletariat, strait-jacketed by a single party, encircled by a propaganda which isolates it, forms a closed society without doors or windows. There is only one means of access, a very narrow one: the Communist Party*.[169]

Sartre also had harsh words to say about the way the PCF operated politically, accusing it of using *persuasion by repetition, by intimidation, by veiled threats, by scornful assertion, by cryptic allusions to evidence that is never produced and by exhibiting so complete and brilliant a conviction that it places itself above all debate*.[170] It is little wonder that Sartre concluded that *the politics of Stalinist communism are incompatible with the honest practice of literary craft*[171] . . . *Since we are free we won't join the watchdogs of the Communist Party*.[172]

Sartre's choice of the word 'watchdogs' (the title of a book by Nizan) was not a coincidence. After Nizan's resignation from the PCF in August 1939 in protest at the Nazi-Soviet non-aggression pact, the PCF leadership had spread the rumour that he was a police spy, an accusation recently reiterated in a book written by a leading Communist attacking existentialism.[173] In July 1947 *Les Temps modernes* published Sartre's robust defence of Nizan,[174] calling on the Communists either to produce evidence for their accusations or to desist from making them. He was supported by an eclectic group of intellectuals, including Aron, Camus, Breton and Mauriac, and the PCF failed to come up with any proof of Nizan's 'betrayal'. *Challenged publicly to produce their evidence, they scattered in all directions reproaching us for never having trusted them and for not being very nice.*[175]

In October and November, Sartre, Merleau-Ponty and Beauvoir scripted and recorded nine half-hour radio programmes on topical issues for a weekly series entitled 'Tribune des *Temps modernes*'. The very first programme on de Gaulle and Gaullism – broadcast days after the success of the Gaullist Rassemblement du Peuple Français (RPF) in the municipal elections – caused a public furore. While Sartre may have respected de Gaulle's role in the Resistance, he nevertheless considered him to be fundamentally a bourgeois, right-wing, authoritarian militarist with strong anti-democratic instincts. The programme not only ridiculed the General's domestic and foreign policies, but also insulted him personally. As a result, Sartre and his fellow-participants were denounced as 'virtual fascists', while the right-wing novelist Paul Claudel (1868–1955) wrote: 'Monsieur Sartre criticizes General de Gaulle's looks. Is he so satisfied with his own?'[176]

The 'de Gaulle affair' also marked the definitive break between Sartre and Aron. Aron had acceded to Sartre's request to join him in a discussion with two Gaullists which was held after the broadcast. During the onslaught against Sartre, Aron said nothing. For Sartre, who had hoped Aron would support him, this was an act of betrayal. *It was from that moment that I understood that Aron was against me politically speaking,* he observed. *For me, his siding with the Gaullists signalled a break.*[177] Aron later recalled that Sartre himself had not responded to his Gaullist opponents. 'He never liked face to face confrontations,' he said, and 'remained undaunted by the insults while I remained silent. Each of us went our own way afterwards.'[178] In fact, Aron soon joined de Gaulle's RPF and started writing for the conservative newspaper *Le Figaro*. It was about this time that Sartre also broke with Koestler who thought that de Gaulle was the best solution for France. The political differences were now so great, according to Sartre, that they could not even go and see a film together. As for the 'Tribune des *Temps modernes*', five more programmes of the nine recorded were broadcast before it was closed down by the Government.

This dispute did not send Sartre rushing into the arms of the Communists – he would not have been welcome anyway, as the PCF's anti-Sartre offensive made clear. Sartre's critique of the Stalinist interpretation of Marxism, his complaint that the Party prevented him from reaching the working class with a rival philosophy, plus his staunch defence of Nizan and merely a qualified defence of the Soviet Union only served to fuel the Party's paranoia and its intense dislike of him. Relations worsened considerably in 1948 with his decision to join a new left-wing organization and the opening of his play *Les Mains sales* (*Dirty Hands*).

In February 1948 Sartre aligned himself with the newly formed Rassemblement démocratique révolutionnaire (RDR), an organization founded by journalists and militants from the revolutionary non-Communist left. The RDR aimed to build a new revolutionary democratic movement open to members of existing parties and members of no party. It offered an alternative to 'the rottenness of capitalist democracy, the weaknesses and flaws of a certain type of social democracy and the limitations of communism in its Stalinist form',[180] with a radical European political perspective based on peace and freedom. *It is not a question of abandoning freedom, not even abandoning abstract bourgeois freedoms*, wrote Sartre. *The first aim of the Rassemblement démocratique révolutionnaire is to link revolutionary demands to the idea of freedom.*[181]

Predictably, the PCF castigated the RDR as a bourgeois, reactionary, anti-Communist outfit, while the French Section of the Workers' International (SFIO) threatened to expel any member who joined it. Sartre threw himself wholeheartedly into RDR activities, writing for its newspaper *La Gauche-RDR*, speaking at public meetings and giving interviews, but the movement failed to grow as its founders had hoped. *We were not very numerous, maybe between 10,000 and 20,000*, Sartre later admitted. *Anyway, it was the embryo of a party and we were attacked as such. In fact, the RDR never got beyond this first phase. Our ideas were very vague.*[182]

The peak of the RDR's activities came in December 1948 with an international rally in Paris that attracted more than 4,000 participants. Sartre spoke and, refusing to side with either superpower, attacked the possible open confrontation between them which threatened the independence and even the very existence of other nation states. Although the RDR began by occupying a neutral position between the United States and the Soviet Union, it was soon seeking funding from American trade unions. Sartre resigned in October 1949 and later recalled: *This was my first political move and I have to say it was not a happy one.*[183]

David Rousset (1912–97), the driving force behind the RDR, later remembered Sartre as a political novice, which is confirmed by Sartre's rather uninspiring contributions to two published political discussions with two other leading members of the group.[184] However, Rousset added that Sartre's 'personal relations with the RDR members were excellent. He was totally at ease with them. He didn't advertise that he was a cultural celebrity. There was even a clear intention on his part to be accepted on an equal footing with everyone else.'[185]

On 2 April *Dirty Hands* opened at the Théâtre Antoine. The play was inspired by the problems experienced by Sartre's ex-students who had joined the PCF, by the assassination of Stalin's rival Leon Trotsky (1879–1940), and the expulsion of the French Communist Jacques Doriot (1888–1945) from the PCF in 1934 for advocating unity between Communists and Socialists (before it became Party policy). The two central characters in the play are Hoederer, the Communist leader and revolutionary realist, and Hugo, an idealist and rebel who is in Hoederer's household with a mission to assassinate him.

Sartre asserted in a contemporaneous interview that although

Dirty Hands was about politics, it was not *in any way at all a political play*.[186] Nor was it didactic. When asked if he was advocating idealism and revolutionary purity, he retorted: *I do not take sides. A good play should pose problems not resolve them . . . I am only concerned, I repeat, with this: can a revolutionary, in the name of effectiveness, risk compromising his ideals? Has he the right to get his hands dirty?*[187]

Camus had attended a rehearsal and while he approved of the play, he was critical of one exchange in which he thought Sartre was suggesting that Hoederer, the Communist leader, was right and Hugo was wrong.

Anti-Communism in France had been given a boost by coverage in the right-wing press of the Communist-inspired waves of strikes in the autumn and by the Communist coup in Prague in February 1948. Many Parisian critics rushed to describe Sartre's play as 'Anti-Communist', claiming that it showed how Communists dealt with dissidents within their ranks and that its denouement was an illustration of Communist opportunism and cynicism. While insisting that his play was not anti-Communist, Sartre later had to admit that *at a certain moment, given the circumstances in which it appears, a play takes on an objective meaning given to it by an audience . . . That means that the play became of its own accord, objectively anti-Communist and that the intentions of the author no longer counted.*[188] With its 625 performances in Paris, 300 in the provinces and many abroad in translation, *Dirty Hands* became Sartre's most popular play.

In January 1949 Sartre engaged in a series of polemical exchanges in the pages of *Combat* with the Hungarian Marxist Georg Lukács (1885–1971). Lukács accused Sartre of having introduced a moral imperative into *Existentialism and Humanism* that was quite absent from *Being and Nothingness*. Sartre denied that he had changed his philosophy – though he reserved the right to do so, as and when his thinking evolved. He then attacked Lukács for having repudiated his early writings and for not waiting until Sartre's fully articulated thoughts on ethics had been published. *It is a peculiar philosophical method that criticizes a moral philosophy which at the time is scarcely even sketched out. Lukács knows perfectly well that I'm currently working on a Moral Treatise.*[189] Sartre had been working on his Moral Treatise on and off since the end of the war, but he would soon abandon it, declaring that ethics was no more than a collection of idealistic tricks to help live the life imposed upon us by the poverty of our resources and the insufficiency of our techniques. The unfinished text was published posthumously in 1983.[190]

In May Sartre met the great American jazz saxophonist Charlie Parker (1920–55) at a club in St Germain. Sartre loved jazz and also classical music, especially Beethoven, Ravel, Stravinsky and Bartók. He played the piano well, often accompanying himself, and frequently played duets with his mother in their flat.

In the summer he holidayed with Dolores in Mexico, Guatemala, Panama, Curaçao, Cuba and Haiti, where he became very interested in voodoo; meanwhile, Beauvoir went to Italy and North Africa with Algren.

At the end of the year, the third part of the *Roads to Freedom* trilogy *La Mort dans l'âme* (*Iron in the Soul*) – extracts of which had appeared earlier in *Les Temps modernes* – was published. The first part covers the period from 15–18 June 1940, while the second part describes the first days in captivity of a group of French soldiers. Although *Iron in the Soul* is considered by many to be the best of the trilogy, it shocked the Right because of its portrayal of French officers abandoning their men and upset the Communists with its depiction of French people as passive and apolitical. In 1950 Sartre published two texts that further estranged him from the Communists, the first on the Soviet camps and the second on Yugoslavia under Marshal Josip Tito (1892–1980).

In January 1949 Sartre attended the Kravchenko trial in Paris. Victor Kravchenko a high-ranking Soviet official who had defected to the West and denounced the Soviet regime in his book *I Chose Freedom* (1946; published in French in May 1947) was suing the newspaper *Les Letters françaises*, which had called him a liar and claimed that his book had been written by the US State Department. Thanks to the testimony of witnesses like Margarete Buber-Neumann, who had been an inmate in both Nazi and Soviet camps, the issue of the Soviet camps burst into in the public domain, although evidence of their existence had been available since the 1930s.

Margarete Buber-Neumann (1901–89) was the daughter-in-law of the philosopher Martin Buber (1878–1965) and the wife of leading German Communist Heinz Neumann (1902–1937) who fled from Germany to the Soviet Union in 1933 where it is believed he was executed without trial as a Trotskyist in 1937. She has written about 'the concentration camps of both dictatorships, the roll calls, the marching uniformed columns, the millions of human beings reduced to slavery; in one, dictatorship in the name of socialism; in the other, for the profit and glory of the master race.'[191]

In January 1950 an editorial signed by Merleau-Ponty and Sartre appeared in *Les Temps modernes*, along with an article by Roger Stéphane on forced labour camps in the Soviet Union.[192] Sartre and Merleau-Ponty conceded that the number of prisoners totalled 10 or possibly 15 million people and they were now forced to conclude that 'there is no socialism when one out of every twenty citizens is in a camp'. However, they rejected attempts to equate the Soviet Union with Nazi Germany and asserted that despite everything the USSR was still on the side of the exploited of the world. The editorial concluded with an attack on David Rousset, who had been a prisoner in the Nazi camps and who had recently launched a public campaign about the Soviet camps. By concentrating solely on the Soviet Union, it said, Rousset was presenting a skewed world view that could only comfort the capitalist West. What about repression carried

Maurice Merleau-Ponty

out by the West? What about unemployment, the treatment of American blacks, the use of forced labour in the colonies, and the waging of colonial wars?

Sartre and Merleau-Ponty had tried to relativize and contextualize Stalin's death camps, but in the eyes of the PCF, which insisted that the camps were merely 're-education centres', they had denied that the Soviet Union was a socialist state and had thereby supported anti-Communist forces. The Party duly stepped up its attacks on Sartre, and the more relaxed links that Merleau-Ponty had until then enjoyed with the PCF became increasingly strained.

Sartre's relations with the PCF worsened with the publication of a preface[193] he wrote to a book sympathetic towards Tito's attempt from 1948 to establish in Yugoslavia an alternative socialist system to the one adopted by the Soviet Union. The break with Moscow had seen Tito – previously Number Two in the world communist hierarchy – condemned as a traitor, a spy and a fascist, and accused of opening up a breach in the anti-capitalist/anti-imperialist front. According to the PCF, Tito's attempts to introduce workers' control were nothing but a ploy to steer Yugoslavia into the capitalist camp. Sartre's preface, peppered with references to the works of Friedrich Engels (1820–95), Karl Marx (1818–83), Vladimir Ilich Lenin (1870–1924) and Rosa Luxemburg (1871–1919) revealed his growing familiarity with Marxism, and he expressed considerable sympathy for Tito's experiment. At the end of the text he concluded: *We have to rethink Marxism, we have to rethink Man*.[194]

In the spring Sartre and Beauvoir travelled to the Sahara and black Africa. They had hoped to meet leaders of the anti-colonialist Révolution démocratique africaine (RDA), but the RDA militants were under instructions from the French Communists to have nothing to do with Sartre, so the meetings never took place.

Back in Paris, Sartre had a series of rows with Dolorès, who had arrived in France with the firm intention of settling there, much to Sartre's irritation and discomfort. Unusually for him, in August he had a showdown with her. Dolorès left and they never met again.

An Anticommunist is a Rat[195a]

When the Korean War began in the summer of 1950 many feared it was a curtain-raiser to World War Three. Sartre and Merleau-Ponty were able to compare their reactions to the war when they met in August. Sartre was confused but relatively unaffected: *My thinking didn't go as far as his, which is what saved me from melancholy*[195]. . . *I didn't believe anything, I was swimming in uncertainty. That was my good fortune. I wasn't even tempted to think that midnight had struck for our century . . . I watched this conflagration from afar and saw only some fire.*[196] But Sartre had no doubt who was responsible: *In this miserable affair, the war is the fault of the feudalists of the South and the American imperialists. But I don't doubt either that the North attacked first.*[197]

The outbreak of hostilities came as a severe blow to Merleau-Ponty. He had been closer to Marxism than Sartre, closer to the PCF and had invested more in the Soviet Union – witness his defence of the Moscow Trials that had so enraged Camus. In

After the Second World War, Korea had been divided at the 38th parallel and by 1947 a pro-Communist regime was established in the north, a pro-American regime in the south. In 1949 the victory of the Communists in China transformed the balance of forces in the Far East and on 25 June 1950 the North Korean army crossed the 38th parallel, aiming to unite Korea under a Communist government. Thanks to the absence of the Soviet representative from the UN Security Council, the UN speedily endorsed the deployment of troops in support of the South. Thus it was that troops from the United States, Britain, Turkey, Australia and other Western allies were dispatched to Korea.

1945 he had viewed the Soviet Union with guarded optimism, but had subsequently become increasingly disillusioned. Shortly before the Korean War began he was reduced to defending the Soviet Union solely on the basis of its revolutionary aspirations. What appeared to be a Soviet-backed invasion of South Korea shattered the last of his illusions, exposing the USSR as an aggressive, expansionist force.

For Merleau-Ponty, as for many others, noted Sartre, *1950 was the crucial year. He thought he had seen the Stalinist doctrine without its mask and it was Bonapartism. Either the USSR wasn't the country of socialism, in which case it didn't exist anywhere and doubtless never would, or else socialism was* that, *this abominable monster, this police state, the power of those birds of prey.*[198] For Merleau-Ponty the only resort was silence, because in any case nobody was listening and the outcome of the war would be decided by brute force.

Sartre devoted most of 1951 to writing another play, *Le Diable et le Bon Dieu* (*The Devil and the Good Lord*), which opened at the Théâtre Antoine on 7 June 1951. Camus had attended the rehearsals and their friendship briefly rekindled. Inspired by a play by the Spanish novelist Cervantes (1547–1616), *The Devil and the Good Lord* is set in the sixteenth century during the Peasants' Revolt. *Goetz, my hero, first of all does evil. Then on the throw of a die, he decides to devote himself, with the same resolution to doing good . . . But the outcome is the same and the same disasters befall him. Why? Because in both cases, his acts are determined by relations with God rather than relations with his fellow human beings.*[199]

In the final scene, Goetz decides that God does not exist and sides with his fellows in the revolt. Unlike Orestes in *The Flies*, Goetz realizes his need for other people and is determined to join with them in the struggle for liberation. *The Devil and the Good Lord* caused a scandal in Catholic circles, but ran continuously until March 1952 with a special 30-performance revival in September. The year 1951 also saw a revival of *The Flies* with

Olga Kosakiewicz (under her stage name Olga Dominique) appearing in the role of Electra that she had created in the 1943 production; but the revival was a complete flop, largely because of poor direction.

That same year Sartre began to edge closer to the Communists. Already in December 1950 he had written a powerful indictment of American foreign policy and expressed in print his conviction that the United States was a greater threat to world peace than the Soviet Union.[200] In 1951 he joined a PCF-led campaign to free Henri Martin, a Communist sailor who had been

Olga Dominique acting in the failed revival of *The Flies*.1951

sent to fight for France against the nationalists in Vietnam and in 1950 had been sentenced to five years' imprisonment for producing and distributing material in France against the Indochina War.

The Communists approached Sartre because of his public pronunciations opposing US foreign policy and because of the consistent, anti-colonial stance *Les Temps modernes* had taken on Indochina. As early as December 1946 an editorial in the review[201] had denounced the conflict in Indochina as a colonial war, claiming that the French were behaving in Indochina just like the Germans during the Occupation and calling for French withdrawal. The PCF calculated that Sartre's involvement in the campaign would generate publicity and hopefully hasten Martin's release.

In January 1952 Sartre presented a petition to Vincent Auriol, President of the Republic, protesting at the treatment of Martin.

Auriol told Sartre that he agreed the sentence was excessive, but could not consider reducing it while the PCF campaigned for his release for fear of being seen to giving in to Communist pressure. The PCF continued its campaign and Sartre edited a book about the case[202] that was published two months after Martin's early release in August 1953.

At the end of May 1952 Sartre holidayed in Italy with Michelle Vian, who had separated from her husband Boris. It was while they were in Rome that they heard about the demonstration in Paris on 28 May protesting against the visit of the American General Ridgway, who had replaced General Eisenhower as Supreme Allied Commander in Europe. Ridgway had been the most senior American soldier in Korea, where, it was (falsely) alleged by the Communists, he had sanctioned the use of chemical and biological weapons. The anti-Ridgway demonstration, banned by the Government, led to violent clashes. There were more than 700 arrests, 50 people were seriously hurt and one demonstrator was killed.

An unavoidable sign of protest on the streets of Paris at the visit of General Ridgway

An indication of the Government's anti-Communist paranoia was the arrest of Jacques Duclos (1896–1975), deputy leader of the PCF, who was found in possession of two pigeons – on the absurd grounds that he intended using them to carry news of the demonstration to Stalin. There followed a more general state clampdown on the PCF, leading one commentator to note that it 'was as though McCarthyism, then at its height in America, had crossed the Atlantic and settled in Paris'.[203]

Sartre was outraged when news of the events reached him. He had been reading a collection of letters and documents relating to Louis Napoleon's bloodless coup of 1851 and found numerous parallels with the current situation in France. He became convinced that the 'bourgeois Right' was preparing a political coup. *It was all these letters that showed me how much shit could be crammed into a bourgeois heart, and at the same time that I was reading about Duclos and the carrier pigeons. The two things merged, both seemed to me to be stemming from the same mentality, even though separated by a hundred years. And then all these things radicalized me and I became a Communist fellow-traveller.*[204] As Sartre wrote elsewhere: *The final links were broken, my view was transformed. An anti-Communist is a rat. I'm not shifting from that and never will . . . After ten years of ruminating, I had come to breaking point and only needed that final straw. In the language of the Church, this was my conversion . . . In the name of those principles that it had inculcated into me, in the name of its humanism and its 'humanities', in the name of liberty, equality and fraternity, I swore to the bourgeoisie a hatred that would only die with me. When I precipitously returned to Paris, I had to write or suffocate.*[205]

Sartre started writing furiously and in July the first part of 'Les Communistes et la paix', ('The Communists and Peace') appeared.[206] Sartre may have moved to being a Communist fellow-traveller, but his frantically scribbled rebuttals of right-wing and far-left criticisms of the PCF came from a position of independence. *The aim of this article is to declare my agreement with the Communists on precise and limited issues, reasoning from* my *principles and not* theirs.[207] In the second part, published in the autumn,[208] Sartre considered the failure of a strike called by the PCF a week after the Ridgway riots. He distinguished between the masses, a collection of isolated and powerless individuals, and the working class, united in a common revolutionary purpose, into which they would be transformed by the catalyst that was the Party.

The publication of the first two parts of The Communists and Peace caused tensions within *Les Temps modernes*. Following Merleau-Ponty's retreat from politics in 1950, Sartre had recruited some new blood to the editorial committee in the summer of 1951. Two of these new recruits, Claude Lanzmann (*b*.1925) and Marcel Péju (*b*.1922) in particular, helped Sartre to re-politicize the review and steer it towards the broadly fellow-traveller orientation that Merleau-Ponty had abandoned. For his part, Merleau-Ponty distanced himself further from *Les Temps modernes*.

It was around this time, as Sartre moved closer to the PCF, that the break with Camus occurred. In 1951 Camus's *L'Homme révolté* (*The Rebel*) was published and after much embarrassment at *Les Temps modernes*, where nobody thought much of it, the critic Francis Jeanson was commissioned to write a review. Sartre urged him not to be too harsh, but Jeanson produced a scathing indictment of the book.[209] Camus was deeply hurt and angry and wrote a cold, impersonal response, not to Jeanson but to his old friend Sartre. It opened extremely formally with '*Monsieur le Directeur*' ('To the Editor').[210]

It was Sartre's turn to be incensed. He replied to Camus,[211] taking him to task for placing himself above the fray and from his lofty vantage point preaching an impotent, idealistic aesthetic of revolt. While he, Sartre, was prepared to make the compromises that political action inevitably required, he accused Camus of resolutely refusing to get his hands dirty. Camus was, in Sartre's eyes, an anti-Communist moralist, strong on general principles but whose evasion of History resulted in a refusal to commit himself on specific issues and campaigns. After a very public playing-out of the dispute, the two men never met again.

In June 1952 Sartre's biography *Saint Genet, comédien et martyre*[212] (*Saint Genet: Comedian and Martyr*) was published. Sartre had first met the French author Jean Genet (1910–86) in 1944. In 1947 he had supported Genet's successful candidature for the Pléiade Prize for his plays *Les Bonnes* (*The Maids*, 1946) and *Haut surveillance* (*Deathwatch*, 1947). In 1949 Sartre had begun writing a preface to Genet's works. Six parts appeared in *Les Temps modernes* (July–December 1950) before the book, now a sprawling 578-page tome, finally appeared. Difficult to classify, *Saint Genet* combines philosophy, literary criticism, existential biography and ethics, as applied to Genet.

Genet was a rough, tough individual, a thief and a homosexual, and Sartre greatly admired him for being 'authentic', for having

Jean Genet in 1950. He was one of the few figures to win Sartre's undiluted admiration

freed himself from his past and made something out of what other people had made of him. Sartre went so far as to describe him as *one of the heroes of these times*.[213] As with *Baudelaire*, *Saint Genet* played with the conventions of biography. Both books are fundamentally constructions using Sartre's own philosophical concerns, most notably individual freedom.

It was also in the summer of 1952 that Sartre started to be active in the Communist-inspired International Peace Movement. For the next four years – with the exception of two plays, *Kean* (1953) and *Nekrassov* (1955) – nearly all Sartre's writing was devoted to political issues, as was a good deal of his time and energy. On 12 December he gave the opening speech at the People's World Congress for Peace in Vienna, arguing that war between the two superpowers was not inevitable and that peaceful co-existence was indeed possible. On his return to Paris, Sartre spoke at a mass meeting at the Vélodrome d'Hiver, where he rejected criticisms that the World Congress was a purely Communist event and maintained that it had been truly extraordinary. *There have been for me three experiences since I was an adult that have given me hope again: the Popular Front in 1936, the Liberation and the Congress of Vienna . . . I bear witness therefore to the fact that the Congress of Vienna is, and will remain, an historic event.*[214]

In April, a month after the death of Stalin, Sartre engaged in a polemical exchange with Claude Lefort (*b.* 1924),[215] ex-Trotskyist and friend of Merleau-Ponty, who had criticized the positions taken by Sartre in 'The Communists and Peace'. In particular he attacked Sartre's views on the revolutionary practice of the working class and the role of the Party, accusing Sartre of leaning towards the democratic-centralist position set out by Lenin in *What is to be Done?* (1902). Merleau-Ponty found the offensive, aggressive tone of Sartre's reply unacceptable and threatened to resign from *Les Temps modernes* unless Sartre cut one particularly violent passage. In May he finally did resign from *Les Temps modernes* over an article that Sartre insisted on including.

Meanwhile Sartre continued to show his commitment to the Peace Movement. He addressed a meeting in Paris where he argued that France's attempt to internationalize the conflict in Indochina at the very time when negotiations had started to end the Korean War, made French policy one of the main causes of international tension.[216]

While Sartre was working closely with the Communists, especially in the Peace Movement, he was starting to seriously question why he had developed such a passionate desire to become an author. He now began to reject the belief that he would find salvation through writing and started to abandon the notion of the immortality of the genius; he discovered the source of his mission to be a writer lay in his childhood. *This is where it all started: to cure myself of a malaise, I invested everything in writing with the result that I've been writing for 50 years.*[217]

In 1953 he began writing about his life up until his mother's second marriage. He called the book *Jean sans terre (John Lackland)*, punning on the French name for King John (1167–1216) of England, who managed to lose so much territory. However, it would appear 10 years later as *Les Mots (Words)*. *The bulk of* Words *was written in 1953. That was when I was doing all that work on myself. At that time all sorts of changes were taking place in me, and in particular I realized that I had been living in a true neurosis since the moment I started writing, even before, from the age of nine until I was fifty. The neurosis was basically like the one Flaubert suffered in his day, in that I believed that nothing was more beautiful, nothing was greater than writing and that writing would create lasting works and that the life of a writer should be understood through his writing. At that time, in 1953, I understood that this was a totally bourgeois viewpoint, and that there were a lot of other things besides writing and that writing had a very different place from the one I had assigned it. From that point of*

view, somewhere around 1953–54, I was immediately cured of my neurosis. And then I wanted to understand, to understand why it was that a boy of nine slipped into that 'neurosis of literature' when other boys were normal. And so I wrote Words.[218]

By now Beauvoir was intimately involved with Claude Lanzmann and for the first (and last) time in her life was living with a man; however, because of the shortage of space in the tiny flat she and Lanzmann shared in the rue Bûcherie, she would often work in the apartment Sartre shared with his mother in the rue Bonaparte. Beauvoir was concerned that her relationship with Lanzmann and Sartre's political commitments (about which she was uneasy) would damage her relationship with Sartre. But not all Sartre's time was spent on politics. He and Michelle Vian were still in a relationship and they holidayed with Beauvoir and Lanzmann in Italy or in the south of France, where Michelle had a house. It was while he was in Venice with Michelle in June that he heard

Ethel Rosenberg (née Greenglass, 1915–53) was a clerk for a shipping company until she was sacked for organizing a strike by 150 women workers. She joined the Young Communist League and became a member of the American Communist Party. In 1939 she married Julius Rosenberg (1918–53), chairman of the Party's Industrial Division, and they held meetings at their apartment. Julius was an inspector at the US Army Signal Corps until 1945 when his membership of the Party came to light. In 1950 Ethel's brother accused Julius of being in a spy ring. The Rosenbergs were arrested, found guilty of espionage, and executed.

that Julius and Ethel Rosenberg, found guilty of passing atomic secrets to the Soviet Union during the war, had been executed. He promptly wrote an article expressing his anger and outrage[219] and *Les Temps modernes* published an editorial on the same topic entitled *American Way of Death.*[220]

The eponymous hero of Sartre's play *Kean* – which opened on 14 November and was adapted from an original work by Alexandre Dumas (1802–70) – was based on the great tragic actor Edmund Kean (1787/90–1833), who performed Shakespeare in London and Paris. Kean became an actor in order to reveal the hypocrisies and posturings of the society that nurtured him, but one of the themes of the play is that he does not know when he is acting and when he is being himself. *The actor 'plays himself' all the time, every second*, wrote Sartre. *It is both a marvellous gift and a curse. He is his own victim, never knowing who he really is or whether he is acting or not.*[221]

In February 1954, after attending a meeting of writers from East and West at Knokke-le-Zoute (Belgium), Sartre was invited by the Russian writers to visit Moscow. He arrived at the end of May for what was to be a very demanding month of talks, interviews, organized visits to universities and factories, meetings, sightseeing tours and banquets. A few days before he was due to leave for France via Stockholm, where he was to attend a Peace Movement meeting, Sartre was taken ill, in large part due to the punishing schedule of his programme, especially the vast quantities of alcohol and rich food he had consumed. Even before setting off for the Soviet Union, Sartre had been suffering from hypertension. Now his blood pressure was even higher and his pulse-rate twice as fast as normal. He was hospitalized for ten days.

It could never be said that Sartre led a healthy life or took good care of himself. He had 'rotten teeth, chipped into yellow and black stumps between which he would stick the stem of his pipe'.[222] He suffered from toothache, but would only go to the dentist when the pain became unbearable. As well as being a heavy smoker (pipe and cigarettes), he was also a heavy drinker. He drove himself hard and, when necessary, used amphetamines to extend his basic writing routine up to 15 hours a day. He took little exercise and now, as he reached his fifties, all this had begun to take its toll.

Nevertheless, Sartre was a fussy eater. *Basically, there are not many things I like to eat. There are things I just won't eat – like tomatoes for example.*[223] He also disliked oysters, shellfish, vegetables, fresh fruit and by the mid 1970s he had more or less given up eating meat. *I ate it for a long time*, he said, *then I rather gave up on it because it made me too aware that I was eating part of an animal.*[224]

Towards the end of his life, when he had become disillusioned with the Soviet Union, Sartre was fairly dismissive about his first trip to Moscow. *I wasn't particularly enthusiastic about what I saw in the USSR. I was shown, of course, what could be shown, but I had a great many reservations.*[225] This is not how it appeared at the time, however. In July *Libération* published five articles based on interviews with Sartre about his impressions of the Soviet Union. The tone can be gauged by the headline of the first article – TOTAL FREEDOM OF EXPRESSION IN THE USSR – while in another Sartre predicted that *Around 1960, before 1965, if France continues to stagnate, the average standard of living in the USSR will be 30 per cent to 40 per cent higher than ours.*[226]

Later he explained away his eulogizing of the Soviet Union by saying that he was too ill to re-read the articles properly, and that in any case they were written by his secretary Jean Cau. However, in August he gave another interview[227] in which he repeated much of what had appeared in *Libération*. Sartre had been flattered by the warmth with which he had been received in the Soviet Union. His rapprochement with the PCF, his involvement in the Peace Movement, his conviction that the United States was the greatest threat to world peace and his fragile health and his own uncertainty about the USSR had led him to suspend his critical faculties and to paint an excessively rosy picture of life in the Soviet Union.

Some 20 years later he recanted: *After my first visit to the USSR in 1954 I lied. Well 'lied' is perhaps a bit strong. I wrote an article that Cau finished off because I was ill – I'd been hospitalized in Moscow – where I said some nice things about the USSR that I didn't believe. I did that partly because I thought that when you have just been a guest somewhere you can't pour shit all over your hosts as soon as you get home, and partly because I wasn't very sure about where I stood in relation to the USSR and my own ideas.*[228] Six months after his visit to Moscow, however, Sartre was elected vice-president of the France-USSR Association. It drew him even further into the Communist orbit, although he still refused to join the PCF.

Sartre's literary output had dried up and indeed in June 1954 he told Beauvoir that he thought literature was *a load of horseshit*. Nonetheless in 1955, besides writing several articles for *France-URSS* and other journals, he wrote *Nekrassov*, a satirical play about political manipulation by the Press. It opened at the Théâtre Antoine at the beginning of June. *Nekrassov is about a conman who passes himself off as a Soviet minister who has defected and who makes sensational revelations to the mass-circulation press just before a by-election.*[229] Sartre insisted his play was *not aimed against the Press per se, but against a certain type of press, and the methods it used for spreading anti-communist propaganda.*[230]

Given the play's subject matter, it is not surprising that it was lambasted by the right-wing press. According to Sartre, some newspapers even refused to accept advertisements for it. He explicitly linked his play to his political activities in the peace movement: at the Vienna Congress, after all, Sartre had been one of the 100 writers who had pledged 'to make our works consistent with our wish for peace and we declare that we shall fight a war in our writings'.[231] In an interview published on the day *Nekrassov* opened, Sartre stated: *I wish to make a contribution as an author to the struggle for peace. We made commitments in Vienna; we must stand by them.*[232]

In June 1955 he and Beauvoir were in Helsinki for another Congress of the Peace Movement. He met Georg Lukács again, with whom he had engaged in the polemical exchange about existentialism in 1949. At this time Merleau-Ponty, who was becoming increasingly annoyed by Sartre's political stance, published *Les Aventures de la dialectique* (*The Adventures of the Dialectic*) in which he attacked Sartre's 'ultra-Bolshevism'.

It was about this time that Beauvoir and Sartre were introduced to Lanzmann's 22-year-old sister Évelyne Rey. Like Olga and Wanda, she was an actress and was soon playing Estelle in a revival of Sartre's *In Camera*. Also like Wanda, Michelle Vian and possibly Olga, she became intimately involved with Sartre.

Beauvoir was known to be Sartre's special and closest companion, but he was playing a complex game of amorous hide and seek, arranging to see the many women in his life at different times so that they would not meet each other. He was particularly drawn to young women and was extremely attentive, making each one feel special in the time he allotted them. He was not bothered if they had a full sexual relationship or not, he simply relished the fact that attractive young women found him fascinating and irresistible.

Most of them accepted Sartre's terms, but Rey resented the secrecy surrounding their affair and wanted to spend more time with him. 'Sartre was too busy,' noted Beauvoir, 'he had too many women, too many other commitments, so he could not give her too much of himself. She suffered because of that . . . it was this very, very great, great friendship she had for Sartre that scarred her enormously. She couldn't handle it that she could not exhibit this friendship in public because he did not want her to.'[233] Rey committed suicide in 1966.

Sartre spent the summer of 1955 in Italy with Michelle Vian, working sporadically on his account of his childhood, while

Lanzmann and Beauvoir holidayed in Spain. Beauvoir's novel *Les Mandarins* (*The Mandarins*) had won the prestigious Goncourt literary prize and with the prize money she bought an artist's workshop overlooking the Montparnasse cemetery in the south of Paris. In September she accompanied Sartre on a two-month visit to China.

Sartre and de Beauvoir in China. 1955

During their stay they were constantly accompanied by official 'guides' and insulated from informal contact with the populace, but Sartre did get to meet the Chinese leader Mao Zedong (1893–1976). However, to his disappointment, the Chairman was not interested in engaging in any substantial discussion. Sartre and Beauvoir both declared they were impressed by the progress the Chinese people had made in eradicating poverty and constructing a new socialist society. *Paradoxically, the Chinese revolution began by driving out of China inflation, poverty, price rises, insecurity, anarchy, local tyrannies, in brief a list of problems which, in the eyes of conservatives, always happens with revolutions . . . In 50 years*

Mao Zedong promises the blossoming of a new civilization.[234] On their way back from China, the couple stopped off in Moscow where Beauvoir was able to sample first-hand some of the hospitality that had laid Sartre low the previous year.

Back in Paris, Sartre continued working on his autobiography and was also adapting a film scenario, *The Witches of Salem*, from the play *The Crucible* (1953) by the American playwright Arthur Miller (1915–2005).

In January 1956 Sartre made his first speech on the struggle for Algerian independence that had begun in November 1954. It revealed his growing familiarity with Marxist methods of analysis and placed the economic mechanisms of French colonial exploitation of Algeria in an historical context stretching from the nineteenth century to the present. Although Sartre was not yet explicitly advocating Algerian independence, he concluded: *the only thing that we can and must try to do – that is today essential – is to fight alongside them* [the Algerian people] *in order to free* both *Algerians and French people from the tyranny of colonialism.*[235]

Sartre's growing familiarity and sympathy with Marxism became clearer the following month when he wrote that Marxism was not just a philosophy but a *climate for our ideas, the environment where they grow.* However he observed that *in France, Marxism has come to a halt.*[236] It was not able to deliver what it promised. *Since the death of bourgeois thought, it is Marxism that has the monopoly of Culture, for it is Marxism alone that allows us to understand people, works and events. Or there at least is Marxism as it should be. Sadly, we have to see it as it actually is.*[237]

In March 1956 Sartre met Arlette Elkaïm, a 19-year-old Jewish Algerian who had written to him with some questions concerning her reading of *Being and Nothingness.* They corresponded briefly and very soon she became another of his mistresses. According to Beauvoir, he was attracted to her because she was very young, very pretty, very intelligent – and shorter than him. Initially, Beauvoir welcomed Arlette into the Sartre/Beauvoir entourage, since Arlette's willingness to do whatever Sartre required, freed Beauvoir and Sartre to pursue their writing. There had always been 'a continuous succession of starry-eyed young women to take care of Sartre, so there was no reason for her to suspect that Arlette would become anything more than another of his sexual playmates and runner of his errands, who would eventually grow tired of his many demands and move on to other interests'.[238] Little did she know.

Sartre, de Beauvoir and Claude Lanzmann dining out in Paris

In July Beauvoir, Lanzmann, Michelle Vian and Sartre holidayed in Greece, Yugoslavia and Italy. In Italy, where Sartre's relations with the Communists were much more relaxed than in France, he learned of the Soviet invasion of Hungary. He was appalled and dismayed. After the exposure of Stalin's crimes at the Twentieth Congress of the Communist Party of the Soviet Union and the beginnings of what many hoped was a process of

The Hungarian Uprising of 1956 began with agitation for reform, to which the police replied by opening fire on the demonstrators. On 24 October some 30,000 Russian troops entered Budapest to 'restore order'; Imre Nagy, who had been prime minister until he was purged, was brought back to head a new government. On 28 October Soviet premier Khrushchev ordered the withdrawal of Soviet forces. To the alarm of the Soviet authorities, Nagy announced his intention to abolish the one-party system and introduce liberal reforms. In the face of what the Soviet leadership considered to be an open, counter-revolutionary revolt, 15 Russian divisions and 4,000 tanks moved into Hungary and surrounded Budapest. After two weeks of bitter fighting the revolt was put down. Some 700 Soviet soldiers had been killed and 1,500 wounded, with between 3,000 and 4,000 Hungarians killed and about 200,000 fleeing abroad.

de-Stalinization in the Soviet Union and eastern Europe, here was the USSR behaving like an aggressive, imperialist power.

On his return to Paris Sartre gave an interview in the course of which he stated: *I condemn absolutely and without any reservation at all the Soviet aggression . . . Regretfully, I am completely breaking all my links with my friends the Soviet writers who have not denounced (or cannot denounce) the massacre in Hungary. I cannot remain friends with the leading faction of the Soviet bureaucracy. Horror is ruling the roost.*[239]

There were harsh words, too, for the PCF, whose leadership had enthusiastically supported the Soviet invasion, arguing that the USSR had heroically saved socialism in Hungary from a fascist counter-revolution. While Sartre did not rule out the possibility of renewing his links with the Soviet Union, *as far as the men who are currently in charge of the French Communist Party are concerned it is not, and never will be, possible to renew relations with them. Each of their sentences, each of their gestures is the culmination of 30 years of lies and stagnation. Their reactions show they are irresponsible.*[240] He signed several petitions protesting against the Soviet invasion and resigned from the France-USSR Association. However, he stayed in the Peace Movement where he proposed a resolution demanding the withdrawal of the Soviet forces from Hungary.

Out in the political cold again, Sartre called for the formation in France of a *sort of new-style popular front whose driving force could be the 'New Left'*; otherwise, he added grimly, *the Left is lost.*[241a] The New Left in France did not materialize; meanwhile a supposedly 'socialist' government was prosecuting the war in Algeria. Soon enough Sartre was to establish himself as the most famous French advocate of Algerian independence.

Marxism and Anti-colonialism

The decade following the Soviet invasion of Hungary was dominated for Sartre by his engagement with the theory and practice of Marxism and his political commitment to the liberation struggles in the developing world, notably Cuba, Vietnam and especially Algeria.

Having broken with the PCF and the Soviet Union over Hungary – at least temporarily – Sartre tried to understand what the invasion said about the USSR and Marxism. In the case of the USSR, he concluded that the repression in Hungary had resulted from the dominance of Stalinist elements within the state apparatus and in his view Communism could extricate itself from its ossification only by a thorough process of de-Stalinization.[241] He saw hopeful signs in Poland, where Wladyslaw Gomulka (1905–82) was attempting to introduce a more pragmatic form of socialism. In January 1957 Sartre visited Warsaw for the première of *The Flies* and wrote a major article entitled 'Marxism and Existentialism' for the Polish journal *Twórczosć*, which appeared later in *Les Temps modernes* as 'Questions de méthode'[242] ('Search for a Method').

In 'Search for a Method' Sartre defined philosophy as *simultaneously a totalization of knowledge, a method, a regulative Idea, an offensive weapon and a community of language.*[243] He then posited three philosophical moments since the seventeenth century – the moment of Réne Descartes (1596–1650) and John Locke (1632–1704), the moment of Immanuel Kant (1724–1804) and G W F Hegel (1770–1831), and finally the appearance of Marx –

with each in turn becoming *the humus of every particular thought and the horizon of all culture. It is impossible to go beyond them for as long as the world has not moved beyond the historical moment that they expressed.*[244]

Since the world had not gone beyond the material conditions which gave rise to Marxism, it remained *the* philosophy of the time and Sartre relegated existentialism to *an ideology, a parasitical system living on the edge of Knowledge.*[245] But Marxism had become stagnant; indeed it was a reflection of the failure of twentieth-century Marxism that it had been unable to account for the lived dimension of human experience in the world that helped bring existentialism into being. According to Sartre, Marxism had been hi-jacked by the Communists who had distorted it, transforming it from a creative revolutionary tool into a closed, rigidly dogmatic stultifying force whereby 'theory' had become pure fixed knowledge and 'practice' merely unprincipled self-justification. *Marxism possesses theoretical bases and embraces all human activity*, he wrote, *but it no longer* knows *anything. Its concepts are* dictates. *Its goal is no longer to increase what it knows but to set itself up a priori as absolute Knowledge.*[246]

By now Sartre and *Les Temps modernes* had also become increasingly vocal over Algeria. His first public intervention on Algeria in January 1956 coincided with Guy Mollet's accession to head the French government. Very soon Mollet had secured 'special powers'; the number of French soldiers in Algeria doubled and by 1957 allegations of the systematic use of torture by the French army as part of its 'pacification policy' were circulating in France.

In May *Les Temps modernes* published Sartre's commentary on a pamphlet in which French conscripts described the torture they had witnessed in Algeria, but it was rejected by *Le Monde* as too violent. In the text we find the two recurrent themes of Sartre's writing on the war at this time, namely the extreme brutality of the Army's campaigns in Algeria and the de facto collusion of the French population in these violations of human rights. The failure of the majority of French people to mobilize against the actions of their army was a constant source of deep disappointment and frustration for Sartre.

In the summer Sartre published the preface to a book on the colonizer and the colonized[247] in which he denounced the oppression, super-exploitation and violence of the colonizer which condemned the colonized to a life of misery and ignorance; in December he appeared as a defence witness at the trial of Ben Sadok who had assassinated the former vice-president of the Algerian assembly, considered by many Algerians to be an arch collaborator. Sadok was found guilty but escaped the death penalty and was sentenced to life imprisonment.

While he was railing against French brutality in Algeria, the passivity of his fellow citizens made Sartre angry and frustrated; he also felt politically impotent and isolated. After the publication of 'Search for a Method' he threw himself into writing *La Critique de la raison dialectique* (*The Critique of Dialectical Reason*). He was working more intensely and frenetically than ever before. No longer pausing, reflecting, crossing out words, tearing up pages and starting again, as was his custom, but writing for hours at a time, racing through one page and on to the next without re-reading it, and

Invaded by the French in 1830, Algeria was subsequently divided into three departments and became constitutionally an integral part of France. By the 1950s the country had a population of around nine million (including about a million Europeans, mainly with French and Italian roots, who had been born in Algeria). On 1 November 1954, just months after the French had been defeated in Indochina, a series of bomb attacks marked the beginning of what was to become a bloody eight-year war of independence waged by Algerian nationalists against the French.

Sartre consults a guidebook on St Mark's Square, Venice. 1957

then on to the next and so on for hours. It was as if he were terrified that if he slowed down he would lose the thoughts that he was so maniacally pursuing in order to capture them and turn them into words on paper.

He was also fuelled by drugs, notably corydrane, a mixture of aspirin and amphetamines that was banned in 1971. The recommended dose at the time was one or two tablets in the morning and again at lunchtime, but when he started on the *Critique*, Sartre was taking 10 at a time and soon it was up to 20. *When I'd taken 10 corydranes in the morning, I was in a state of complete bodily surrender. I perceived myself through the movements of my pen, my imagination and my thoughts which were forming . . . There were the ideas that I was formulating in my mind at the very moment I was writing them down and there was the writing itself, all this going on at the same time.*[248] In addition to swallowing huge quantities of corydrane, Sartre was knocking back a tube of orthodrine a day. Not surprisingly, by evening he was exhausted, his gestures were uncertain and he had a tendency to say one word instead of another, much to the consternation of Beauvoir and his friends.

In March 1958 he wrote an article for *L'Express* that was prompted by the torture and arrest in 1957 of Henri Alleg, the editor of the newspaper *Alger républicain*, whose account of his detention had been published as *La Question* a month earlier. As a result of Sartre's article, that issue of *L'Express* was banned and three weeks later so was *La Question*.

By 1958 the failure of the politicians to find any solution to the Algerian crisis had strengthened the hand of the Army, which was increasingly operating as an autonomous force and had drawn up plans for a military *coup d'état* in mainland France. In May 1958 de Gaulle made it known that he was willing to return as head of state, which he duly did on 13 May. Sartre was convinced that de Gaulle was unfit to be the head of a democratic republic and that his assumption of power (with the backing of the military and European civilians in Algeria) would only boost the pro-colonial camp in France and Algeria.[249] Sartre and Beauvoir joined a huge anti-de Gaulle demonstration in late May and Sartre continued to denounce torture in Algeria.

In September a referendum was held in France on a proposed constitution for a Fifth Republic. In an article written on the eve of the referendum,[250] Sartre argued that de Gaulle had been brought to power by the military and that the referendum was just a device to ratify an illegal seizure of power. He further accused de Gaulle of trying to blackmail the French population and called for a rejection of the constitution. In the event, the constitution was endorsed by some 80 per cent of the electorate and the Gaullist Fifth Republic was born. Sartre was cast into despondency, while Beauvoir took the view that the French had just repudiated themselves and everything that she and Sartre believed in, in a mass collective suicide.

Sartre's health continued to deteriorate. His demented drug-fuelled work schedule started to take its toll and his problems with his balance, his difficulty in walking and his stumbling over words persisted. He finally and reluctantly agreed to consult a doctor who told him that if he continued in the same vein, he would be dead in six months. *I saw that I was damaged goods*, wrote Sartre. *I was never afraid. But I stopped. For two months, I don't think I did anything.*[251]

De Gaulle had come to power, but the war in Algeria continued and indeed initially

An anti-war cartoon exposes the threat of military power in France. 1958

intensified. In May 1959 Sartre contacted Francis Jeanson – who had savaged Camus's *The Rebel* in *Les Temps modernes* and who for two years had been running a clandestine support network for the Algerian Front de libération nationale – and gave an interview to Jeanson's underground newspaper, *Vérités pour . . .*[252]

He finished writing his *Critique* in the summer and after spending time in Rome with Beauvoir, returned to Paris to complete a new play called *Les Séquestrés d'Altona* (*The Condemned of Altona*). Delayed for a year because of Sartre's poor health, it opened in September. Starring Serge Reggiani in the lead role, and featuring Wanda and Évelyne Rey, the play contained a number of themes familiar from Sartre's earlier work, notably a closed world (echoes of *In Camera*), a man who cannot confront reality and who lives in bad faith, and the way human relations

are dominated by conflict (*In Camera* again). Like *Bariona* and *The Flies, The Condemned of Altona* had a political dimension, this time using a series of flashbacks to examine the actions of a German officer, Frantz, in 1945 and 1959. By highlighting the issue of torture, Sartre wanted to encourage the audience to draw parallels between Frantz's (or France's) situation and that of soldiers returning from Algeria who had to confront their involvement in inhuman and barbaric acts.

Early in 1958 Sartre had a nasty shock when he received a tax bill for 12 million francs. He

Evelyne Ley (left) in her role in *The Condemned of Altona*

had made money, but had always been hopeless at managing it. He spent a lot on travelling and gave money to his mother, friends and acquaintances. He was also an absurdly generous tipper, which he explained by the fact that waiters depended exclusively on tips, so it was his responsibility to ensure they did not go short. In order to pay off the debt, Sartre agreed to write a screenplay for a film on Sigmund Freud for the American film director John Huston (1906–87). He would be paid $25 million.

In the autumn of 1959 Sartre and Arlette travelled to Ireland to meet Huston, but it was not a great success. The director kept disappearing for lengthy trips on horseback and complained that Sartre's screenplay was far too long (a film based on the scenario would have run for seven hours). He also thought that Sartre was the most stubborn and dogmatic person he had ever had to work with and that it was impossible to have a conversation with him, since you could never interrupt him and he drowned you in a torrent of words. Sartre, for his part, complained that it was *impossible to hold his* [Huston's] *attention for five minutes: he no longer knows how to work and avoids reasoned argument.*[253] In the end the film was made based on a new screenplay and Sartre, who was nonetheless paid, managed to secure the removal of his name from the credits.

The following year, 1960, began badly. In January Camus died in a car crash. Although Sartre and Camus had not spoken since their break in 1952, they remained aware of one another through their writings and political statements,[254] which revealed sharp differences over Algeria.[255] As Sartre wrote in an article published after Camus's death: *We had a falling out, he and I. A falling-out is nothing – even if we were never to see each other again – just another way of living together without losing sight of each other in this narrow little world that we have been given.*[256]

In the spring the first volume of *The Critique of Dialectical Reason*, a monster of a book, longer even than *Being and Nothingness*, was published. Written, as we have seen, between 1957 and the beginning of 1960, it was the fruit of Sartre's reflections on Marxism. They had begun in the early 1950s when he was drawing close to the PCF. In the 1940s Sartre had contested Marxism from without (as in, for example, 'Materialism and Revolution'). Now, however, his starting point, as he made clear in *Search for a Method* (published now as the first part of the *Critique*) was that Marxism was untranscendable; it was *the* philosophy of his time. One of the issues that Sartre was exploring was how to reconcile the dialectical method of (undogmatic) Marxism with existentialism.

The *Critique* is an uncompromising (and difficult) work of philosophy. It attempts to 'lay the ontological foundations of the truth of Marxism in order to allow Marxism to take account of itself, that is to say, to understand its own pre-suppositions.'[257] *I have said it and I say it again that the only viable interpretation of History was historical materialism . . . Marxism is History itself becoming aware of itself.*[258]

Sartre wanted to extricate Marxism from the impasse in which it found itself, then to develop it, strengthen it and adapt it to contemporary conditions. As he observed in 1975: *You cannot explain a multinational company using Marxist terms from 1848. You need to introduce a new notion that Marx had not anticipated and which is therefore not Marxist in the simple sense of the term.*[259]

Sartre's starting point is that we live in a world characterized by scarcity and violence, and within this context he seeks to understand how it is that History, the result of free praxis (the activity of groups and individuals who organize conditions with a particular end in view), turns back on the agents of History, who then become set in an inhuman necessity that reduces them to the objects of an historical process. In the *Critique* Sartre uses a number of key notions to explore this phenomenon – for example, seriality, group-in-fusion, pratico-inert – *notions which it seems to me come from Marxism, but which are different.*[260]

Analysing the French Revolution in July 1789, Sartre shows

how a heterogeneous collection of individuals (he gives the example elsewhere of a bus queue) can transform itself into a different type of group when the interests that the individuals have *in common* become a *common interest*, when communication between the members of the group shifts from indirect to direct communication and when the group is aware of the existence of other groups with opposing interests and therefore with whom they are de facto in conflict. In short, this collection of disparate individuals transforms itself into a single organism. He describes this process as the transition from *seriality* to *group-in-fusion*.

When this occurs in the case of a revolutionary uprising, the members of the group-in-fusion experience a sense of solidarity with one another, a sense of belonging to a new collective formation. In order to survive against other antagonistic groups, the group-in-fusion needs to consolidate its organization. Discipline is introduced in the name of the cause and soon the group becomes an end in itself and eventually becomes *practico-inert*: characterized by bureaucracy, conservatism and frequently repressive measures against 'traitors' in its ranks. The second part of the *Critique*,[261] which was to have applied Sartre's analysis to concrete historical examples, remained incomplete and was published posthumously.

Sartre and Beauvoir had spent a month from the end of February in Cuba, where they were deeply affected by the euphoria of revolution that had overthrown the US puppet leader Fulgenico Batista (1901–73) a few months earlier. Sartre immediately perceived developments in Cuba as a living example of a group-in-fusion where people are linked together in a collective enterprise and, what was more, an undogmatic one. In the *Critique* he had written that in the process of the formation of the group-in-fusion the individual changes and becomes a new person, and this was now happening in Cuba: *A lucid practice has changed things in Cuba, including the very notion of 'man'.*[262]

Sartre and Beauvoir in conversation with Fidel Castro (left) and Che Guevara. Sartre initially greatly admired the vitality and achievements of the Cuban Revolution but later became disillusioned.

While there were similarities with his trips to China and the Soviet Union – visits to co-operatives, factories and schools, discussions with workers and students – there was a striking absence of formality, hierarchy and ponderous rhetoric. Sartre and Beauvoir met the young leading figures of the revolution, including Ernesto 'Che' Guevara (1928–67), who had been appointed head of the national bank; and spent three days with the leader of the revolution, Fidel Castro (*b*. 1927). On his return, Sartre wrote a series of 16 articles lauding what he had seen in Cuba, which were published in the summer in a popular newspaper.[263] These articles, the performance of his new play, the publication of the *Critique* and a preface written for a new edition of Nizan's *Aden Arabie*, meant that in 1960 Sartre was once again back in the limelight on the literary and cultural stage.

After a trip to Yugoslavia in May (where Sartre met Tito), it was back to France where he was once again active over Algeria. In an interview published in the summer[264] he argued that the French Left should support the Front de libération nationale (FLN), the leading force in the fight for Algerian independence, and September saw the publication of a text signed by 121 intellectuals, including Sartre, advocating the right for soldiers to refuse to fight in Algeria.

The publication of this text coincided with the opening of the trial of some 20 members of Francis Jeanson's FLN support network, but by now Sartre was on a two-month trip to Brazil where he was making speeches on Algeria and in praise of the Cuban revolution. A letter purportedly from Sartre was read out at the trial in which he said that he would have been willing to provide active support for Algerian militants if Jeanson had asked him to, although the letter had in fact been composed by colleagues at *Les Temps modernes* on the basis of a telephone conversation with Sartre.

On the Algerian front, Sartre was no longer restricting himself to denouncing colonialism and bemoaning the passivity of the French population, he was now using his fame to openly back those who refused to fight in Algeria and he was publicly supporting 'the enemy', the FLN. He was becoming a hate figure for many supporters of Algérie Française (Algeria remaining part of France) and at a right-wing demonstration in October the marchers chanted 'Shoot Sartre!'

In 1961 Sartre uncharacteristically agreed to accept a prize – the Omenga Prize in Milan in recognition of his work and struggle against the Algerian War – and donated the million francs of prize money to Algerian prisoners. He and Beauvoir went to Antibes, where they heard about the abortive American invasion of Cuba at the Bay of Pigs. This prompted Sartre to give a newspaper interview attacking American imperialism.[265] It was in Antibes that he and Beauvoir learned of the death from a heart attack on 4 May of Merleau-Ponty. In October *Les Temps*

General De Gaulle giving a public address in Algeria. 1958

modernes published Sartre's tribute to the man with whom he had co-founded the review and who, for many years, had been Sartre's political mentor.[266]

Meanwhile the political situation in Algeria was evolving. De Gaulle had realized that the economic and military costs of the war (as well as international condemnation of France's conduct) far outweighed any advantage that 'victory' might bring. He started looking for a way out. Nevertheless the hostilities continued, now complicated by the creation in February 1961 of the Organisation armée secrète (Secret Army Organization) or OAS, a right-wing terrorist group with close links to the French Army. The OAS was committed to using any means to keep Algeria French. In July Sartre's flat in the rue Bonaparte was bombed, but the damage was minimal.

Towards the end of the year Sartre was approached by Frantz Fanon (1925–61), the psychiatrist, theorist of decolonization and revolution, and unofficial ambassador of the FLN. He was asked to write a preface for Fanon's last and greatest work *Les Damnés de la Terre*[267] (*The Wretched of the Earth*). In this preface, the most violent text he ever wrote, fired up by what he had seen in Cuba and seething about France's behaviour in Algeria, Sartre argued that not only was revolutionary violence necessary to counter the inherent violence of colonialism, but it was through violence that the colonized threw off the colonizer's definition of him as a sub-human and asserted himself as a human being.

Sartre later explained the context in which the preface was written: *We were in a difficult position, given that, despite everything we were fighting against France and with the Algerians, who didn't care much for us even though we were on their side. That put us in a pretty special situation which is expressed in the text – a situation where we felt uneasy, of great violence and where, because it was easier, we adopted an intransigent attitude. I found it disagreeable to be against my country.*[268]

Sartre again took to the streets on the Algerian question in November and December, including one silent protest against the violent repression of a peaceful demonstration by Algerians in Paris on 17 October when at least 200 demonstrators were killed. (The head of the Paris police at that time was Maurice Papon, who would be found guilty in 1998 of complicity in 'crimes against humanity' for his involvement in the deportation of French Jews during the Second World War.)

In January 1962 Sartre's flat in the rue Bonaparte was again bombed and this time the damage was much more substantial; although nobody was injured, many of Sartre's manuscripts were destroyed. But the Algerian crisis was now moving towards a resolution. In February against a backdrop of OAS terrorist actions, including attempts to assassinate de Gaulle, a ceasefire was declared and in June Algeria finally became independent.

Sartre deeply regretted the fact that it was his arch-enemy de Gaulle who had been instrumental in securing Algerian independence rather than a mass popular movement or action by the French Left, which he had described in 1960 as *a worm-infested, stinking rotting corpse.*[269] This explains his low-key response to

Algerian independence. *I do not consider that our action was particularly effective*, he observed. *As far as the Algerian War is concerned, we did what we had to do and that's all.*[270]

In June 1962 he and Beauvoir undertook the first of nine trips they were to make to the Soviet Union in the next four years. Because of the French Socialist government's prosecution of the war in Algeria, Sartre had given up on the French Socialist Left, and he still hadn't forgiven the PCF for its support for the Soviet Union's intervention in Hungary. But he had convinced himself that the USSR had entered into a new stage of genuine de-Stalinization.

In March he was elected vice-president of the Congrès européen des écrivains (European Congress of Writers), which had been organized by intellectuals close to the Italian Communist Party (PCI). Sartre was keen to support those usually young, undogmatic writers and artists (known as the 'oppositionists') in the Soviet Union who were struggling to break free from their Stalinist cultural heritage. In the course of his trip to the Soviet Union, he met the Soviet leader Krushchev and engaged in numerous discussions with oppositionist writers. He was back again in July to address a peace congress on the need to extend the notion of peaceful co-existence to the realm of culture and to make literature from different countries freely available to all. In this spirit he advocated, somewhat naively, *a programme to be proposed to all nations: the end to all cultural protectionism, the publication of all important works . . . in all languages under the control of men of culture.*[271]

At the very end of the year, Sartre and Beauvoir were back in Moscow again, where he promoted the project of an East – West writers' community. However, when he returned once more in July 1963, Kruschev had initiated a clampdown and at a reception in his dacha in Georgia attended by Sartre, the Soviet leader denounced Western writers as the henchmen of capitalism, a theme reiterated at a conference in Leningrad in

August which castigated Western art and culture for its decadence and corruption.

In October Sartre visited Prague as a guest of the Czechoslovak Writers' Union. He confirmed that as a socialist he recognized that there were many unwholesome aspects of Western society, but he refused to condone the attacks at the Leningrad conference, which dismissed Western authors such as Marcel Proust (1871–1922), James Joyce (1882–1941), Franz Kafka (1883–1924) and Sigmund Freud (1856–1939) as decadent.

Sartre's frequent trips to the Soviet Union were motivated by a desire to build bridges between writers in the East and the West and to support the progressive 'oppositionists', but there was also a more personal reason. He had established an amorous liaison with the 40-year-old Léna Zonina, his cultivated Russian translator and guide. Sartre probably had no idea that Zonina also worked for the Soviet authorities, writing official reports on him.[272]

Zonina had been forced to leave university in the 1940s because she was the daughter of an 'enemy of the people' and Jewish. As a result of her past and the precariousness of her current post, her affair with Sartre had to be conducted with the utmost discretion, although Beauvoir was aware of it. Indeed, the fact that Beauvoir and Sartre were seen as a couple helped to keep the affair a secret.

In July 1963 Sartre wrote a preface to the writings of Patrice Lumumba (1925–61),[273] the first prime minister of the Democratic Republic of Congo (June–September 1960), who was forced out of office during a political crisis and assassinated in 1961. It has been described as 'perhaps the best text by Sartre on the problems of revolution in the Third World and its contradictions'.[274] However, more attention was paid to his long-awaited autobiography. *Words* was published in *Les Temps modernes* in the autumn of 1963[275] and in book form the following year. It was dedicated to Madame Z., a reference to Lena Zonina, who would translate the book into Russian.

As we have seen Sartre began thinking about an autobiography in 1953 when he was politically close to the PCF. *Thrown into the atmosphere of action, I suddenly saw clearly the sort of neurosis that had dominated my whole life hitherto.*[276] The 'neurosis' to which Sartre referred was that *basically was like the one Flaubert suffered in his day, in that I believed that nothing was more beautiful, nothing was greater than writing and that writing would create lasting works and that the life of a writer should be understood through his writing.*[277] Indeed it was more than this. *Through a need to justify my existence, I had turned literature into an absolute.*[278] Now in the 1960s – as he grappled with Marxism (in the *Critique*) and sought to contribute to the process of liberalization in the Soviet Union – he turned his back on literature, but wryly and self-consciously used the medium of literature *to understand why it was that a boy of nine had succumbed to that literary neurosis while other boys were normal.*[279] As he explained to Beauvoir, *it was a way of saying goodbye to a certain type of literature and I had to produce it, explain it and take my leave of it. I wanted to be literary in order to show the error of being literary.*[280]

Words is scarcely a conventional autobiography: 'facts' are in short supply and some are wrong. Rather than offering a chronological account of his childhood, Sartre uses what he calls in the *Critique* the *progressive-regressive method*. In order to explore the development of his existential ideas, which he locates in the circumstances of his own childhood, he shifts between the 'I' of the child and the 'I' of the late-middle-aged adult in his exploration of existential notions and attitudes which he locates in the circumstances of his childhood. Overall, Sartre wanted to emphasize the significance of early conditioning, but equally importantly to show that by becoming aware of our conditioning we can go beyond it and realize ourselves. *Words* was very well received on the whole, although his wounded mother objected that Poulou had understood nothing of his childhood.

Sartre may have bid adieu to literature with *Words*, but in

October 1964 there were rumours he was being considered for the Nobel Prize for Literature. He informed the Swedish Academy that he did not wish to be involved, but on 22 October they announced he had been chosen for 'his oeuvre which, in the spirit of freedom and the search for truth that it represents, has had a huge influence on our times'.[281]

Sartre and de Beauvoir in conversation in her apartment. 1964

Sartre refused to accept the award or the 250,000 kroner ($53,000) prize money, giving his reasons in a press release: he had always refused official honours (like the Légion d'honneur at the Liberation) and had also never wanted to become a member of the Collège de France, the pinnacle of intellectual recognition in France. Writers, he argued, take responsibility for their actions and their political positions as writers, not as members of an institution. *The writer must therefore refuse to allow himself to be transformed into an institution.*[282]

In addition, he explained that he was committed to the *peaceful co-existence between two cultures, East and West* and, although he had been raised in a bourgeois family and culture, his sympathies lay with socialism and the East. To accept the honour would have compromised his position, since the Nobel Prize was perceived by many as reserved for writers from the West, plus a few conservative, dissident rebels in the East.

At the end of 1965 Sartre caused something of a stir in his entourage when he applied to legally adopt Arlette Elkaïm as his daughter. He had no dependents and did not want his royalties to pass to the State on his death. Arlette was already often mistaken for his daughter. Furthermore, her mother was dead and she had lost contact with her own family. The adoption was granted on 18 March, the month in which Sartre's latest play opened. It was an adaptation of *The Trojan Women* (415 BC) by the Greek tragic poet Euripedes (*c.*484–406? BC). As Sartre made clear, the play was *a condemnation of war and of colonial expeditions in particular.*[283]

Although Algeria was now an independent state, he signed a petition that was sent to the Human Rights Commission at the United Nations drawing its attention to the threat to human rights and personal safety in that country. But Sartre's main political preoccupations remained events in the Soviet Union and, increasingly, opposition to America's involvement in Vietnam. In March 1965 Sartre cancelled a series of lectures he was due to give at Cornell University in protest at the American escalation of the war in Vietnam, in particular the bombing of the North, and in May he sent a message of support to the organizers of a 'teach-in' on Vietnam at Boston University.

Meanwhile, in the Soviet Union a brief spell of liberalism had given way to repression, as was evident from the sentencing of two dissident writers – Andrey Sinyavski (*b.* 1925) and Yuli Daniel – to seven and five years respectively for 'damaging the social and political regime of the USSR'. But when Sartre (and Beauvoir) visited the Soviet Union in May 1966, the dissident writer Alexander Solzhenitsyn (*b.*1918) – whose book *The First*

Circle had been condemned by the Soviet authorities the previous year – refused his offer of a meeting. Sartre had publicly regretted that Boris Pasternak (1890–1960) had been awarded the Nobel Prize for Literature in 1958 before Mikhail Sholokhov (1905–84), author of *Quiet Flows the Don* (1934), who was awarded the prize six years later. Sholokhov was tainted in Solzhenitsyn's eyes because he toed the party line and even received the Stalin Prize in 1941.[285] Sartre soon realized he had made a political gaffe by praising a Stalinist writer and not pointing out that Pasternak – whose *Doctor Zhivago* (1957) was banned in the Soviet Union – had been forced to refuse the Nobel Prize. The following year Sartre refused to attend a meeting of the Soviet Writers' Union, unwilling to appear to condone the sentencing of Sinyavski and Daniel or the several attempts to silence Solzhenitsyn.

In July 1966 Sartre and Beauvoir agreed to a request from the English philosopher Bertrand Russell (1872–1970) to join an international tribunal on American war crimes in Vietnam. Before the first session of the Tribunal, held in London in October, Sartre and Beauvoir spent the early autumn in Japan where they received an enthusiastic welcome. The trip was a great success, except for the food which Sartre found inedible, though he developed a great liking for Japanese whisky. In Tokyo and Kyoto he gave three lectures on the role of the intellectual, entitled 'Plaidoyer pour les intellectuals' ('A Plea for Intellectuals').[286]

At the first session of the Russell Tribunal, Sartre was elected executive president. In that same month he also helped launch an appeal announcing the creation of a National Vietnam Committee in France and chaired a conference in Paris organized by the Co-ordinating Committee Against Apartheid. In January 1967 he travelled to London to meet other members of the Russell Tribunal and the following month he presented to the French media the report of the first commission of enquiry which had visited Vietnam.

In Stockholm for the Russell Tribunal, Sartre, the chairman is seated behind Vladimir Dedijer. 1967

Russell was keen for the Tribunal to be based in Paris, but the French authorities refused to grant a visa for the chairman, the Yugoslav Vladimir Dedijer (1914–90). Sartre wrote to de Gaulle saying he hoped there had been a mistake. Not at all, replied the President, referring to Sartre as *Mon cher maître*, a formal term of address used for writers. This infuriated Sartre. *It's to underline, I believe, that he is addressing the writer, not the chairman of a tribunal that he doesn't want to recognize. I am only* 'maître' *for the waiters who know that I write.*[287] De Gaulle insisted that justice was the monopoly of the State and that 'Lord Russell and his friends' had been granted no power, had no international mandate and were therefore unqualified to deliver any judicial verdict. The Tribunal finally opened in Stockholm in May where, in the absence of the nonagenarian Russell who was too fragile to travel, Sartre and Beauvoir were its most famous members.

Early in 1967 Sartre revived his interest in the Middle East and the vexed question of Arab-Israeli relations. He had been an unconditional supporter of Israel's right to exist since the end of the Second World War, but in recent years he had become sensitive to the plight of the Palestinians. In February 1967, accompanied by Beauvoir and Claude Lanzmann, he travelled to Egypt as part of a cultural-political visit, where he spent three hours talking to President Gamal Nasser (1918–70). Nasser and Sartre both agreed that there appeared to be little hope of agreement between the Palestinians and the Israelis over the question of the Palestinians' right of return, and at the time Sartre had no intimation that Nasser envisaged a war against Israel. He and Beauvoir then flew directly from Egypt to Israel, where they were joined by Arlette.

Beauvoir and Sartre met the Defence Minister Moshe Dayan (1915–81) and the Prime Minister Levi Eshkol (1895–1965). As he had done in Egypt, Sartre was careful not to take sides but to raise questions and above all listen to what people told him. Back in France he added his name to a petition stating that 'the State of Israel is currently manifesting proof of an obvious desire for peace and sang-froid'.[288] This upset a great many pro-Palestinians, including Fanon's widow who insisted that Sartre's preface be removed from any further editions of *The Wretched of the Earth*. In June *Les Temps modernes* published an informative special issue on the Arab-Israeli situation,[289] but by the time it appeared, Egypt and Israel were at war.

By the end of the 1960s Sartre's international reputation was at its zenith. He had been awarded (but refused) the Nobel Prize for Literature and over the past decade he had been received by political leaders in China, the Soviet Union and Soviet bloc, the Third World and the Middle East, while his anti-colonialist and anti-imperialist stance was recognized throughout the world.

But in France it was a rather different story. Sartre was no longer fashionable. Existentialism was seen as rather passé and Sartre's interrogations of Marxism had not had the comparable impact of the works of the 'structuralist Marxist' Louis Althusser (1918–90). His ideas were being challenged, primarily by 'structuralists' who rejected his insistence on freedom and the creative power of human beings (albeit now reconfigured through his engagement with Marxism) and his refusal, as they saw it, to recognize that every human being is enmeshed in complex networks of meaning and structures that shape their lives and thinking.

Sartre disliked face-to-face confrontations and was reluctant to acknowledge that he might learn anything from anybody else, so he largely avoided engaging in debate with this new generation of thinkers, which included, besides Althusser, the linguist and critic Roland Barthes (1915–80), the psychoanalyst Jacques Lacan (1901–81), the philosopher and historian Michel Foucault (1926–84), the 'deconstructionist' philosopher Jacques Derrida (1930–2004). Instead, Sartre restricted himself to sniping at them occasionally in a language that now sounded very out-dated. He dismissed structuralism as *the refusal of History*, adding that *behind history, of course, it is Marxism that is being attacked. It's all about constituting a new ideology, the final barrier that the bourgeoisie can erect against Marx.*[290]

Sartre was no longer an important player in the intellectual life of Paris, but anyone who thought he was going to fade away quietly into his dotage was in for a big surprise.

May 1968, Maoism and Flaubert

In March 1968 an article appeared in *Le Monde* noting that 'The French are bored, young people are bored, General de Gaulle is bored.'[291] Two months later France was brought to a standstill by the biggest wave of civil unrest in her history. As the conflict between French students and the university authorities escalated, so too did the violent clashes in the streets of Paris where students manning barricades and armed with cobblestones confronted police wearing full anti-riot gear.

Confrontation between students and police on the Boulevard Saint Germain, Paris. 1968

On 6 May Sartre signed a brief declaration in support of the rioting students;[292] then a lengthier one two days later in which he and other signatories called for the students to be given moral and material support.[293] The movement continued to gather momentum, with the students demanding the re-opening of the Sorbonne (which the authorities had closed), the release of arrested 'comrades' and the withdrawal of the police from the Latin Quarter.

Interviewed on Radio Luxembourg (RTL) on 11 May, Sartre explained that the students did not want to lead the same bourgeois lifestyles as their parents, nor were they interested in merely tinkering with the system. They wanted a radical overhaul. *The only relationship they can have with this university*, he said, *is to smash it and in order to smash it there is only one solution, to take to the streets.*[294]

A few days later, the students marched to the Renault car factory at Billancourt in south-west Paris. The following day, sympathetic and disgruntled French workers went on strike in such numbers that France started to grind to a halt: public transport stopped, banks closed, factories were occupied and goods – including petrol and cigarettes – were in short supply.

On 20 May Sartre interviewed Daniel Cohn-Bendit (*b.* 1945), a leading figure in what became known as *les événements* ('the events')

Student leaders Danny Cohn-Bendit and Tariq Ali

of May 1968. Cohn-Bendit had been portrayed in the bourgeois Press as a mindless, dangerous agitator, while the PCF leadership (whom Cohn-Bendit had described as 'Stalinist filth') accused him of being a 'German anarchist'. In stark contrast, Sartre generously provided Cohn-Bendit with a platform to air his views. He also praised the spontaneity of the student movement, saying it had *put imagination in power*.

On the day this interview was published,[295] Sartre addressed a packed audience at the Sorbonne, now occupied by the students. In his element, he answered questions on the continuing viability of the dictatorship of the proletariat, the meaning of democracy in a class society, the relevance of the student movement to the Third World, and the reasons for the decline of the traditional Left in France.[296] In June he attacked the elitist French university system and its teachers, in particular his erstwhile friend Raymond Aron, whom he accused of trotting out the same lectures year after year. Aron was typical of those academics who were accountable to nobody and refused to engage with or be challenged by their students.[297]

A week later, however, at the end of June, Sartre realized that the student-worker protest had almost fizzled out. *In some ways, the movement has failed*, he wrote. *But it only failed for those who believed that revolution was on the agenda, that the workers would follow the students to the end, that the action that began at Nanterre and the Sorbonne would result in a social and economic apocalypse that would result not only in the collapse of the regime but the disintegration of the capitalist system . . . That was a dream and Cohn-Bendit, for example, did not believe it.*[298]

Although Sartre backed the student-worker movement, he failed to grasp its full significance at the time: *I was with the student movement. I wrote articles, spoke on the students' behalf on RTL and went to speak with the people who were occupying the Sorbonne. But basically I didn't understand it.*[299] However, he did understand the reactionary nature of the PCF, which he accused of objectively siding with de Gaulle, betraying the 'May revolution' and – through its domination of the trade union confederation – of doing everything possible to prevent contact between workers and students.[300] A year later, he described the PCF as *the largest conservative party in France.*[301]

Meanwhile developments in Czechoslovakia resulted in Sartre breaking once and for all with the Soviet Union. Alexander

Dubcek (1921–92) had become First Secretary of the Slovak Communist Party in January 1968 and in April his reform programme (known as the 'Prague Spring') was gathering pace. Alarmed at what was happening in its own backyard, the Soviet Union decided to put a stop to it and in August Russian tanks rolled into Prague. It was like Hungary all over again.

Sartre was in Rome when he heard of the Soviet invasion. *It is because I have deep respect for the history of the Soviet Union and because I am in no way anti-Communist, that I feel I have a duty to condemn unreservedly the invasion of Czechoslovakia*, he told an Italian newspaper. *Today the Soviet model has no validity, suffocated as it is by the bureaucracy.*[302] On a visit to Czechoslovakia in November/December, he expressed support for the Czech liberalization movement and argued that it *proved the possibility of another road to socialism.*[303]

A break with the PCF; a break with the Soviet Union. In 1969, after eight months of reflection, Sartre also broke with the role of the intellectual, which he had embodied since the Liberation. At a meeting in February to protest at the expulsion of several university students, he was passed a note asking him to make his contribution short. *I realized from the start that I had no business there.*[304] It now troubled him that he might be asked to support a cause solely because of his celebrity status, it made him feel that he was an outsider. It seemed to him that the intellectual could no longer merely claim solidarity from the sidelines with those engaged in struggle. The important lesson that he learned from May 1968 was that the intellectual had to actively engage in the struggle.

An opportunity to put this new notion of *the revolutionary intellectual* into practice came in April 1970 when he established links with the French Maoist organization La Gauche prolétarienne (The Proletarian Left). The French Minister of the Interior described it as 'the most dangerous of all the far-left groups' citing its claim to be responsible for no fewer than 90 violent acts of sabotage and damage to property.[305] The Maoists asked Sartre to become *directeur* of their newspaper, *La Cause du peuple* (*CDP*), their two previous editors having been arrested and imprisoned. Sartre happily agreed.

The moment he assumed responsibility for the paper, Sartre vigorously defended it, claiming it allowed workers to express their anger, hatred and indignation, but also their needs and aspirations. In his view it was the only newspaper that allowed the true voice of the people to be heard, spreading the experiences of the struggle to the workers who were atomized and alienated by capitalism. However, he later said that he also felt that the paper sometimes fell into triumphalism and workerism.

When Sartre aligned himself with the Maoists he was not in political agreement with them any more than they were with him, but he was soon engaging in regular philosophical and political discussions with their leadership and his respect for them and their aspirations increased. He wholeheartedly approved of those Maoists who had abandoned their studies to take up jobs in factories – it chimed perfectly with his notion of *the revolutionary intellectual*. This practical experience offered Sartre hope that it was possible to go beyond the kind of intellectual he had described in Japan in 1965 as *suspect in the eyes of the working class, a traitor to the dominant class, a fugitive from his own class, yet unable to free himself completely from it*.[306]

Sartre admired the Maoists for their espousal of revolutionary violence – which was essentially symbolic – and for the moral underpinning of their actions. When Paris Metro fares were increased, for instance, Maoist militants stole thousands of Metro tickets and handed them out to the workers. Similarly, in Paris one Christmas they raided a luxury store in broad daylight and distributed stolen food to the poor of the suburbs.

Despite his advanced age and frail health, Sartre also participated

in several Maoist-inspired actions. *Before getting me to take part in a political action* [the Maoists] *always take great care to ask me if I agree with it, discuss it with me and, if necessary, amend the original plan.*[307]

On two occasions in June, he and other intellectuals sold the *CDP* on the streets at a time when mere possession of a copy of the newspaper could result in a jail sentence. He was arrested but released without charge.

Sartre waits for his court appearance at the Palais de Justice. 1970

In October 1970, due to appear as a witness at the trial of Alain Geismar (one of the Maoist leaders), Sartre went to the Renault car plant instead. Outside the factory gates he addressed the workers, denouncing the bosses and calling for the unity of workers and intellectuals. A photograph of Sartre haranguing them from an upturned oil-drum appeared in newspapers and on TV screens all over the world.

In December 1970 he was the chairman of a popular tribunal. It concluded that the managers of a coal mine in northern France had been responsible for the deaths of 16 miners in an underground explosion. In June he supported a tribunal calling for a public trial of the police, which the authorities immediately outlawed. In February 1971 Sartre took part in an illegal occupation of Sacré-Cœur basilica in Paris to protest against police brutality and in February 1972 he was smuggled into the Renault works where he attempted to hold a meeting in protest at a crackdown on political activity at the factory.

However, Sartre was not consulted when the Maoists kidnapped the head of personnel at Renault a month later. It was a response to the fatal shooting of a Maoist militant by a security guard at the factory and Sartre's reservations are evident from a statement issued shortly afterwards. He stated simply that *those who were responsible for it* [the kidnapping] *certainly saw their action as a normal response to the ruthless repression that reigns at Renault.*[308]

In May 1971 Sartre and the novelist Maurice Clavel (1920–79) endorsed the launch of the Liberation News Agency by Jean-Claude Vernier (*b*.1943), a leading member of the Maoists. The agency's main aim was to undermine the monopoly of the 'bourgeois press' and to support progressive journalists working within it. It proved so successful that Vernier, Sartre and Clavel decided to transform the Liberation News Agency into a daily newspaper to be called *Libération*. Sartre put about $40,000 of his own money into the project. Tape-recordings of wide-ranging discussions between Sartre, the clandestine Maoist leader Benny Lévy (1945–2003), who used the pseudonym Pierre Victor, and the left-wing journalist Philippe Gavi were published in 1974, the proceeds going to *Libération*.[309]

In his autumn years, Sartre was enjoying the most radical period of political commitment of his lifetime, but he also found time to write a mammoth study of the nineteenth-century novelist Gustave Flaubert. Sartre had read Flaubert as a child, returning to him at the École normale, then again during the Occupation, and there are references to him throughout Sartre's work. Around 1954 he had agreed with the Communist Roger Garaudy (1910–2001) that he would write an existentialist analysis of Flaubert if Gauraudy wrote a Marxist one. Sartre had written about a thousand pages before abandoning the project.

Despite recognizing that he and Flaubert shared the same neurosis about the primacy of literary creation, Sartre was both attracted to, and repelled by, the nineteenth century novelist who, he said, represented *the exact opposite of my own conception of literature; a total disengagement and a certain idea of form, which is not that which I admire . . . he began to fascinate me precisely because I saw him in every way as the contrary of myself.*[310]

In January 1969 he took up the Flaubert book again and began to rewrite it. This also meant returning to his punishing cocktail of corydrane, tobacco and alcohol. Sartre's aspiration was that *the reader simultaneously feels, comprehends and knows the personality of Flaubert, totally as an individual and yet totally as an expression of his time.*[311] In January 1971 the first two volumes of *L'Idiot de la famille* (*The Family Idiot*) were published, followed by a third in 1972. Although this already totalled almost 3,000 pages, two more volumes were promised.

Sartre knew that he had several unfinished works and unfulfilled promises. He had abandoned the treatise on morality announced at the end of *Being and Nothingness*; the fourth volume of the *Roads to Freedom* never appeared; nor, in his lifetime, did the second volume of the *Critique*. This time, however, he was determined that the projected fourth and fifth volumes of *The Family Idiot* would be published. *I will never abandon what I have been doing for so many years*, he said. *I will complete it because it would be absurd not to.*[312] This, however, was not to be.

In June 1973 tragedy struck. He had lost the use of his right eye when he was a child and now, aged 67, a triple haemorrhage at the base of his other eye rendered him almost blind. Hopes that medical intervention might alleviate his condition were dashed when specialists confirmed the damage was irreversible. For Sartre, the man who in *Being and Nothingness* had philosophized about 'the gaze', would never gaze again. Fortunately, he was surrounded by close friends who could assist him with everyday tasks, but his life as a writer as he had defined it was over.

Sartre had always associated seeing and writing, even claiming they were inescapably interlinked. As he had written in his diary as long ago as November 1939: *I'm stopping for now, I cannot manage any longer to think about anything because my eyes hurt. I have never felt so strongly that I* think *with my eyes.*[313] Or, as he told an interviewer after he had gone almost totally blind: *It seems to me that the act of writing to form letters by upstrokes, downstrokes, curves, etc. is the* form *of thinking.*[314]

When this blindness occurred and I realized that I would never be able to write again (I had been writing 10 hours a day for 50 years and they were the best moments of my life), when I understood that it was all over for me I was very affected and I even though about killing myself. But then I didn't even try. You see, I'd been so happy all my life – I had been, I was until then, a man, a character so constituted to be happy that I wasn't going to suddenly change. I carried on being happy out of habit.[315]

Sartre moved out from his flat in the Boulevard Raspail where he had lived since the bomb attack on his mother's apartment in 1962 and found a larger one on the Boulevard Edgar Quinet. It had a lift and a spare room, which meant he would not have to be alone at night. Sartre's many ailments – from his blindness to the onset of diabetes and the drowsiness caused by his medication – severely restricted his level of activity and he was frequently withdrawn and in low spirits.

However, although initially devastated by his blindness, Sartre soon bounced back to explore new ways of expressing himself. *I can no longer either read or write*, he said. *My life as a writer is over. However, I can still speak. This is why my next project, providing funding can be found, will be a series of television programmes in which I shall attempt to speak of the 75 years of this century.*

Sartre hoped to take advantage of the liberalization of the French state media and embarked on this project with his friends Beauvoir, Benny Lévy and Philippe Gavi. The series was to be called *75 ans d'histoire par ceux qui l'ont fait* (*75 Years of History By Those who Made It*), but in September 1975 it was abandoned due to political opposition, most notably from the Prime Minister Jacques Chirac (*b.*1932), and because of alleged financial, technical and administrative difficulties.[316] Disappointed but undeterred, Sartre continued to explore new ground, experimenting with a different form of intellectual collaboration.

Benny Lévy ('Pierre Victor'), a stateless Egyptian in his thirties, was a complex character and his role in the final years of Sartre's life is a controversial one. He had been the main inspiration for and driving force behind the Proletarian Left and it was during Sartre's involvement with the Maoists that the two men had met. In 1973 it was Lévy who had ordered the dissolution of the Maoist network, much to the fury of many rank-and-file activists. Lévy's friendship with Sartre had survived the dissolution of the Maoist movement and after Sartre went blind, Lévy would often visit and read to him, a task previously assumed mainly by Arlette and Beauvoir. In the autumn of 1973 Lévy became Sartre's secretary. He now had a salaried job, which entitled him to a permit allowing him to live in France legally, though he remained stateless. After Valéry Giscard d'Estaing (*b*.1926) was elected as President of the Republic in May 1974, Sartre wrote to him about Lévy's situation and received a handwritten reply. It is an indication of Sartre's influence that Lévy's naturalization followed shortly afterwards.

Those who approve of Lévy's role in Sartre's life at this juncture like to emphasize how this young man (who knew Sartre's *œuvre* intimately and had unbridled admiration for the 70-year-old) set out to establish a lively, combative rapport of equals which helped to revitalize the elderly philosopher. Together the two men embarked on a project that included philosophical discussions on the theme of 'Politics and Freedom' and which were tape-recorded and transcribed by Arlette.

However, some of Sartre's closest friends, especially those who had known him for a long time, were scandalized by Lévy's behaviour. He had the audacity to address Sartre using the informal '*tu*' ('you') rather than the more respectful '*vous*', which even Sartre and Beauvoir had always used. Lévy treated the now frail Sartre as if there was nothing wrong with him, challenging him and provoking him intellectually, even when Sartre appeared to be exhausted. In fact, Lévy's growing importance in Sartre's life made those around him very uneasy, especially Beauvoir, who began to feel threatened and marginalized.

Sartre's friends came to the conclusion that Lévy was exercising an undue influence over the old man and had, in effect, hijacked him, selecting what he would read for his own ends and imposing his own views on him. In short, they thought Lévy was controlling Sartre and using him as a mouthpiece for his own ideas. By now Lévy had switched allegiance from Mao to Moses and had returned to his Jewish roots, immersing himself in the Talmud and the Torah. He had one other ally in the Sartre entourage, namely Arlette. She was of a similar age and also had a Jewish background, and Lévy had started giving her Hebrew lessons.

Whatever misgivings Sartre's friends may have had about Lévy's role in his life, Sartre was extremely positive about it. He had always regarded writing as a solitary exercise – even though he and Beauvoir regularly commented on each other's work in manuscript – but now he was engaged in a collective act of creativity: *a tape-recorded dialogue . . .a real discussion between two real people with their ideas that they are developing . . .This is something completely new; we don't know how it will finish.*[317]

In the past Sartre had been reluctant to acknowledge a debt to anyone, but now he lavished praise on Lévy. *It will be* better written *by two than if the same ideas had been written by one person*, he said, *expressing better the totality of what each one thinks, which is ultimately what* we *think: this involves a* unity *between us, a sort of new way of thinking.*[318]

Nevertheless, Sartre was aware of the unease that his relationship with Lévy was generating. *Either I am an old fool whom you are manipulating or I am a great man who you think will give you food for thought*, he told Lévy. *Those are two possibilities. And then there's a third one, which is the best: that we should be equals.*[319] That Sartre should consider Lévy his equal further infuriated his friends.

Despite his failing health, Sartre had not abandoned international politics. In December 1974 he travelled to Stuttgart and visited Andreas Baader (1943–77), the leader of the notorious Red Army Faction (RAF) – known in the press as the Baader-Meinhof Gang – who was on his fourth week of hunger strike in prison. At a press conference afterwards, Sartre said that while he disapproved of the RAF's activities, he also condemned the conditions under which the militants were being held, which included torture through sensory deprivation.

In a similar spirit, Sartre travelled to Portugal in April 1975 to find out what life was like after the overthrow of the fascist regime. Accompanied by Beauvoir and Lévy, he met students, workers and writers. In the course of 1975 Sartre denounced the repression of intellectuals in Czechoslovakia, repression in the Soviet Union (especially the Ukraine) and the death sentence passed on 11 antifascist militants in Spain. In May the following year he was joined by 50 Nobel prize-winners in a campaign to secure the release of Mikhail Stern, a political prisoner in the Soviet Union and in June 1979 he was reunited with his erstwhile friend from his days at the École normale, Raymond Aron, who, like Sartre, was active in a campaign on behalf of the Vietnamese boat people. Sartre's blindness had not stopped him travelling and besides his trips to Portugal and Spain, he also visited the south of France and Italy.

Sartre turned once again to the vexed question of the Middle East. He still supported a solution that would guarantee the right of Israel to exist, while addressing the grievances of the Palestinians. At a ceremony at the Israeli embassy in Paris in November 1976, when he was awarded an honorary degree from the University of Jerusalem, he declared: *I am as much pro-Palestinian as I am pro-Israeli and vice versa.*[320]

Old friends Raymond Aron and Sartre are briefly reunited, during a campaign for the Vietnamese boat people. Andree Glucksman looks on.

In 1979 he and Lévy organized a colloquium in Paris on the Middle East. It was attended by Arab and Israeli intellectuals, but the event was not a success. The Palestinian intellectual Edward Said (1935–2003) described Lévy as coming across as 'a Left Bank intellectual, part-thinker, part-hustler' and 'sensed that he was a law unto himself, thanks no doubt to his privileged relationship with Sartre (with whom he occasionally had whispered exchanges), and to what seemed to be a sublime self-confidence'.[321] As for Sartre, Said wrote that 'Sartre's presence, what there was of it, was strangely passive, unimpressive, affectless. He said absolutely nothing for hours on end . . . I tried to make conversation with him but got nowhere. He may have been deaf, but I'm not sure. In any case, he seemed like a haunted version of his earlier self.'[322]

In March 1980 *Le Nouvel Observateur* prepared to publish three dialogues between Sartre and Lévy, which provoked fury among

Sartre's entourage. Beauvoir's response to these discussions – in which Sartre appeared to deny some of his earlier philosophical notions – was one of despair, fury and consternation. The text 'had nothing to do with the "plural thought" that Sartre had spoken of in *Obliques*. Victor [Lévy] did not express any of his own opinions directly. He had Sartre assume them while he, by virtue of who-knows-what revealed truth, played the part of grand inquisitor. The tone and the arrogant attitude he adopted towards Sartre disgusted all Sartre's friends who saw the text before its publication. Instead of helping Sartre enrich his thought, Victor was pressurizing him into denying it.'[326]

Despite attempts by Beauvoir and others to prevent publication, Sartre insisted that he wanted the dialogues to be published and telephoned the editor of *Le Nouvel Observateur* to this effect, adding that none of his friends, including Beauvoir, understood how his thinking had developed.

The dispute between Lévy (and his main supporter and Sartre's

Sartre with de Beauvoir, in April 1980, shortly before his death

heir Arlette) and Sartre's old friends (led by Beauvoir) was in part a conflict between two generations, each wishing to appropriate Sartre. Indeed, Beauvoir's final book chronicles this last decade of Sartre's life in distressing detail and includes nearly 400 transcribed pages of her interviewing him about his life. This was no doubt an attempt to reassert her closeness to Sartre, to remind the world of their half-century together, and to snatch Sartre from the clutches of not only Lévy but also Arlette, with whom she would later clash over issues of copyright and publication rights.

On 20 March 1980, while his friends fought over him, Sartre was rushed to hospital with a pulmonary oedema. He slipped into a coma on 15 April and died two days later. He would have been 75 in June.

On 19 April an estimated 50,000 people lined the Paris streets as Jean-Paul Sartre's funeral procession made its way from the Broussais Hospital to Montparnasse Cemetery, not far from the apartment where he had spent the last years of his life. His body was cremated, as he had requested, and the ashes were buried in the cemetery. On 14 April 1986, six years after his death almost to the day, Beauvoir died. They share a grave in Montparnasse with the simple inscription JEAN-PAUL SARTRE 1905–1980, SIMONE DE BEAUVOIR 1908–1986.

Conclusion

In 1971, in reply to the question – 'Have you no worries at all about how posterity will judge you?' – Sartre coolly replied: *None at all. Not that I'm convinced that it* [posterity's judgement] *will be positive.* A hundred years after his birth and a quarter of a century after his death people are still discussing his work and evaluating his legacy.

Sartre continues to provoke both admiration and fascination – as well as criticism and opprobrium – just as he did during his lifetime. In France, while it is true that he has many admirers, there is a powerful negative current in the wave of newspaper and magazine articles currently being published to coincide with the centenary of his birth. However, this critical mood is largely absent beyond France's borders. Today, Sartre is more appreciated outside France than he is in France itself.

There are various reasons for this. Some French people have never forgiven Sartre for his 'anti-French' activities: for supporting the nationalists fighting France in Indochina and especially his support for the Front de libération nationale (FLN) during the Algerian War; for his consistent refusal to embrace 'bourgeois democracy'; for his rejecting the Légion d'honneur and the Nobel Prize; and for remaining an anti-establishment figure – and therefore, in some eyes, a negative role model – until the very end of his life. Then there are those within the universities who positively resent the fact that Sartre secured an international reputation as a philosopher without ever having held a post in a university philosophy department; indeed, without ever having been employed in a university at all. They find it hard to accept that a mere secondary school teacher should have achieved so much in the fields of literature and philosophy and have acquired such fame as an intellectual.

But what are Sartre's achievements today? In terms of quantity and an ability to write in variety of genres, Sartre's output during his lifetime remains unsurpassed. Then there are the works published after his death – his diaries written during the Phoney War, his notebooks on ethics, two volumes of his letters to Beauvoir, a scenario for a film on Freud, a second volume of the *Critique of Dialectical Reason* and a biography of Mallarmé, not forgetting the 400 pages of interviews with Beauvoir which appeared in 1981 in her *Adieux*. Little wonder, perhaps, that Sartre is the subject of the biggest ever exhibition staged at the Bibliothèque nationale (March–August 2005).

While it would be foolish to claim that Sartre's appeal is as great as it was in the immediate post-war period, all of his works have been in print since they first appeared and most are available in paperback. A hundred years after his birth, Sartre's philosophy is still studied, his novels and biographies are still read and his plays are still performed. On a more academic level, Sartre remains one of the most commented upon French writers. Between 1945 and 1985 some 600 works on Sartre were published and each year sees the publication of some 300 articles on Sartre in academic journals, some of which are linked to groups of Sartrean scholars in the Americas and throughout Europe and the Far East.

Sartre was the last philosopher to try to create a system and he never baulked at tackling extraordinarily ambitious projects. One thinks of his attempt to marry existentialism and Marxism in the *Critique* and his desire to write an existentialist ethics. While it is true that in the 1960s existentialism was largely eclipsed by structuralism (and then poststructuralism), leading members of that new generation of thinkers acknowledged their debt to

Sartre. The philosopher and historian Michel Foucault (1926–84) referred to the generation of *Les Temps modernes* as 'our model for existing', while the philosopher Gilles Deleuze (1925–95) wrote of Sartre always being there as an intellectual who changed the situation of the intellectual. Although existentialism is no longer as fashionable as it was, its emphasis on freedom, choice and responsibility still provides a compass to help us find our way through the demands, pitfalls and contradictions of life.

From the Liberation it was Sartre who personified the committed intellectual. At first, in the late 1960s, it was *the classic intellectual* and then, in the early 1970s, *the revolutionary intellectual*. Although Sartre's position as *the* committed French intellectual was unrivalled for some 30 years, little of his legacy in this respect is evident in France today, since the role of the intellectual has undergone a radical transformation. Sartre was an intellectual of the printed word, the mass meeting and to some extent, the radio. Today, French intellectuals rely primarily on television to reach their public and there is a close, some might say incestuous, relationship between publishing houses, writers and intellectuals and the television networks. French intellectuals today have largely abandoned the idea of campaigning on behalf of a particular group, nation state or organization and instead have opted to defend the 'non-ideological' notions of 'human rights'. However, it is interesting to note that when the sociologist Pierre Bourdieu (1930–2002) took to the streets to support the public sector strikers in 1995, many hailed him as 'the new Sartre'.

Linked to the accusation that Sartre's espousal of the *committed intellectual* or *revolutionary intellectual* is *passé* – or even 'dangerous' – is the widely held view that he made mistakes. Sartre stands accused of having committed 'huge errors of analysis and incoherence' (Annie Kriegel) and of having made 'monumental political errors' (Olivier Todd). Most of these accusations focus on his positive comments about the Soviet Union in the 1950s and his support for the Cuban Revolution. Although it is impossible to endorse his claim in 1954 that there was complete freedom of expression in the USSR, this negative view of Sartre needs to be placed in context and counterbalanced with those political statements for which he deserves credit.

In the early 1970s, prompted by the publication of Alexander Solzhenitsyn's *The Gulag Archipelego*, there was a violent reaction against Marxism and Communism to which a number of former leftists contributed (some of whom had been sympathizers of Sartre). As the traditional Left versus Right political paradigm was replaced by a 'totalitarian' versus 'anti-totalitarian' one, Sartre found himself castigated as an apologist for totalitarianism. What his critics generally overlooked was that Sartre had denounced the camps as early as 1950. They also disregarded his consistent support for initiatives which seemed at the time to promise liberation and freedom, for example the moves towards de-Stalinization in the Soviet Union, the Castro experiment in Cuba, Tito's Yugoslavia and Dubcek's attempts to establish 'socialism with a human face' in Czechoslovakia. What is also left out of the equation is the degree to which Sartre's critics during the Cold War underplayed the extent of America's overt aggression, its subversion of regimes and its support of ruthless dictatorial regimes across the world. These Cold War warriors also glossed over the issue of racial segregation which Sartre explicitly addressed in his play *The Respectful Prostitute*.

Nor is Sartre given sufficient recognition for other political positions he adopted, notably his anti-colonialism, his balanced position on the Arab-Israeli conflict and also, more contentiously, his pro-Resistance activities during the Occupation. Also, Sartre and *Les Temps modernes* were among the first to oppose French attempts to crush the independence movement in Indochina. His support for the movement of national liberation in Indochina in the 1940s and 1950s did not, however, prevent Sartre from supporting the cause of the Vietnamese boat people in the early 1970s (they were fleeing the regime established by the forces he had earlier supported). Over Algeria, Sartre was the most visible and the most famous French intellectual to denounce the French army's systematic use of torture; and he supported the independence movement, as a result of which he became the object of a campaign of vilification and his flat was bombed twice. Sartre was an early supporter of the state of Israel, but soon became a defender of the rights of the Palestinians. He rejected the anti-Zionism of the Maoists in the early 1970s and worked consistently for a just and peaceful settlement that could only come from negotiations between the two communities.

Sartre never claimed to have been a resistance fighter during the Occupation, even if this was how others sometimes described him. It should be remembered that only a tiny proportion of the French population was active in the Resistance and the accusation that Sartre 'could have done more' also applies to millions of others. Perhaps his post-war commitment was in some sense a compensation for not having been more active during the war, but it remains beyond any doubt that he was consistently opposed to the German Occupation and to the collaborationist Vichy regime, as he demonstrated in his writings and in his plays *Bariona* and *The Flies*. He wrote nothing during the Occupation to contradict this position.

Jean-Paul Sartre should be given credit for his unique contribution as a philosopher, a dramatist, a novelist, a biographer, an essayist and a polemicist. Furthermore, he deserves our admiration for his willingness to speak out on behalf of the oppressed and for his optimistic belief that a better world was possible. Part of the excitement he generated in his lifetime came from his courageous commitment to questioning everything: not only his own ideas but his very identity; to embrace the tensions between the person he had been, the person he was and the person he wanted to become. It is this constant search for authenticity, combined with his prestigious and varied literary and philosophical output that makes him one of the most dynamic and exciting intellectuals of our age.

Notes

1 Sartre, *Les Mots* (Gallimard, 1964), p. 29

2 Ibid., p. 13

3 Ibid., p. 11

4 Ibid., p. 10

5 Ibid., p. 6.

6 Ibid., p. 23.

7 Ibid., p. 196.

8 Ibid., p. 24.

9 According to *Les Mots* this happened when he was seven, but in a letter written in 1925 Sartre says it was when he was five. (see R. Hayman, *Writing Against*, Weidenfeld and Nicolson, 1986).

10 Sartre, *Les Mots*, p. 84.

11 Ibid., p. 36.

12 Ibid., p. 37.

13 Ibid., p. 61.

14 Ibid., p. 66.

15 Ibid., p. 69.

16 Ibid., p. 62.

17 A. Cohen-Solal, *Sartre* (Gallimard, 1985), p. 55.

18 Sartre, *Les Mots*, p. 104.

19 Ibid., pp. 180–183.

20 Archives of the Lycée Henri-IV, quoted in M. Contat and M.Rybalka, (eds) *Jean-Paul Sartre: Œuvres romanesques* (Gallimard, Bibliothèque de la Pléiade, 1981), p. xxxviii. [Hereafter Sartre, *Œuvres romanesques*]

21 Sartre, *Les Mots*, pp. 184–5.

22 Interview with J. Gerassi, quoted in Sartre *Œuvres romanesques*. p. xxxviii

23 S. de Beauvoir, *La Cérémonie des adieux* (Gallimard, 1981), p. 186. [Hereafter *Cérémonie*]

24 J. Gerassi, *Jean-Paul Sartre: Hated Conscience of His Century* (University of Chicago Press, 1989), p. 57.

25 Ibid., p. 58.

26 'Jacques Guillemin' (J-P Sartre), 'Jésus la Chouette', *La Revue sans titre*, No. 2 (10 February 1923), No. 3 (25 February 1923), No. 4 (10 March 1923), reproduced in J-P Sartre, *Écrits de Jeunesse* (Gallimard, 1990), pp. 60–135.

27 Gerassi, op. cit., p. 61.

28 Ibid., p. 63.

29 Sartre quoted in Gerassi, op. cit., p. 63.

30 Sartre quoted de Beauvoir, *Cérémonie*, p. 196.

31 Sartre, 'Paul Nizan', preface to P. Nizan, *Aden Arabie* (Maspero, 1960), in J-P Sartre, *Situations IV* (Gallimard, 1964), p. 144.

32 Sartre quoted de Beauvoir, *Cérémonie*, p. 178.

33 Sartre, 'L'Ange du Morbide', in Sartre, *Écrits de Jeunesse*, pp. 44–49.

34 Sartre, 'La Semence et le Scaphandre', in Sartre, *Écrits de Jeunesse*, p. 140.

35 Georges Lefranc, quoted in J.-F. Sirinelli, *Génération intellectuelle* (Fayard, 1988), p. 268.

36 Georges Canguilhem quoted in C. Bonnefoy, 'Rien ne laissait prévoir que Sartre deviendrait "Sartre"', *Arts* (11–17 January 1961).

37 Quoted in Cohen-Solal, *Sartre*, p. 86.

38 R Aron, *Mémoires* (Julliard, 1983), p 32.

39 G Canguilhem, quoted in Cohen-Solal, *Sartre*, p. 107.

40 R Aron, quoted in Cohen-Solal, *Sartre*, p. 105.

41 Cohen-Solal, *Sartre*, p. 97.

42 Quoted in Sirinelli, *Génération intellectuelle*, p. 503.

43 Beauvoir, *Cérémonie*, p. 476.

44 Sartre, 'Paul Nizan', p. 146.

45 Ibid., p. 147.

46 A Astruc and M Contat, *Sartre* (Gallimard, 1977), p. 34–35.

47 F Jeanson, *Sartre dans sa vie* (Éditions du seuil, 1974), p. 235.

48 Aron, quoted in Sartre, *Œuvres romanesques*, p. xlvii.

49 Sartre, 'La Légende de la vérité', *Bifur*, No. 8 (1931), pp. 77–96; reproduced in M Contat and M Rybalka, *Écrits de Sartre*, (Gallimard, 1970), pp. 531–45. [Hereafter Écrits de Sartre]

50 Astruc and Contat, *Sartre*, p. 49.

51 Sartre, *Œuvres romanesques*, p. 1736.

52 S de Beauvoir, *La Force de l'âge* (Gallimard, 1960), p. 37.

53 Beauvoir, *Cérémonie*, p. 427.

54 Gerassi, op. cit., p. 116.

55 *Sartre*, op. cit., p. 44.

56 Sartre, 'La Transcendence de l'ego: Esquisse d'une description phénoménologique', *Recherches philosophiques*, Vol. 6 (1936–37; printed August 1937), pp. 85–123.

57 Sartre, *Carnets de la drôle de guerre, Septembre 1939–Mars 1940*, (Gallimard, 1995), p. 273. [Hereafter, Sartre, *Carnets*]

58 Ibid., p. 273.

59 Troupe Matthews, quoted in Gerassi, op. cit., p. 108.

60 Astruc and Contat, *Sartre*, pp. 53–4.

61 Sartre, *Carnets*, p. 275.

62 Ibid., p. 184–5.

63 Beauvoir, *La Force de l'âge*, p. 250.

64 Ibid., p. 263.

65 Quoted in Sartre, *Œuvres romanesques*, p. li.

66 Beauvoir, *La Force de l'âge*, p. 224.

67 P Gavi, J-P Sartre, P Victor, *On a raison de se révolter* (Gallimard, 1974), p. 23.

68 Beauvoir, *La Force de l'âge*, p. 284.

69 Gerassi, op. cit., p. 134.

70 Ibid.

71 Sartre, 'Le Mur', *La Nouvelle Revue française*, No. 286 (July 1937), pp. 38–62.

72 Sartre, 'La Chambre', *Mesures*, Vol. 3, No. 1 (15 January 1938), pp. 119–49.

73 Sartre, 'Intimité', *La Nouvelle Revue française*, No. 299 (August 1938), pp. 187–200 and No. 300 (September 1938), pp. 381–406.

74 S de Beauvoir, *A Transatlantic Love Affair: Letters to Nelson Algren* (New York, 1998), p. 208.

75 Sartre, *La Nausée* (Gallimard, 1938), p. 126.

76 Ibid., p. 125.

77 Ibid., p. 215.

78 Sartre, *Esquisse d'une théorie des émotions* (Hermann, 1939).

79 Sartre, 'Une idée fondamentale de la phenomenology de Husserl: L'Intentionalité', *La Nouvelle Revue française*, No. 304 (January 1939), pp. 129–131.

80 Sartre, *Le Mur* (Gallimard, 1939); including three stories that had already appeared: 'Le Mur' ('The Wall'), 'La Chambre' ('The Room'), 'Intimité' ('Intimacy') and two hitherto unpublished texts: 'Erostrate' and 'L'Enfance d'un chef'.

81 Contat and Rybalka, *Écrits de Sartre*, pp. 69–70.

82 *La Nouvelle Revue française*, No. 293 (February 1938), pp. 323–28 and *La Nouvelle Revue française*, No. 309 (June 1939), pp. 1057–1061.

83 *La Nouvelle Revue française*, No. 299 (August 1938), pp. 292–301.

84 *La Nouvelle Revue française*, No. 305 (February 1939), pp. 212–32.

85 *La Nouvelle Revue française*, No.302 (November 1938), pp. 842–45.

86 Most of these reviews and review articles have been reproduced in J-P Sartre, *Situations I* (Gallimard, 1947).

87 Gerassi, op. cit., p. 140.

88a Sartre, 'Autoportrait à soixante-dix ans', in Sartre, Situations X, (Gallimard, 1976), p. 180

88 Sartre, Letter to Louise Védrine **(late August)**, *Lettres au Castor et à quelques autres*, Vol 1 (Gallimard, 1983), p. 268. [Hereafter *Lettres* Vol 1]

89 Sartre, Letter to Louise Védrine (2 September 1939), *Lettres* Vol 1, p. 272.

90 Sartre, *Carnets de la drôle de guerre*, (Gallimard, 1995).

91 Sartre, 'Autoportrait à soixante-dix ans', pp. 179–180.

92 Beauvoir, *Cérémonie*, p. 489.

93 Sartre, *Carnets*, p. 244.

94 Ibid., p. 293.

95 Ibid.

96 Sartre, *Œuvres romanesques*, p. lvi.

97 Sartre, 'Journal de Mathieu', *Les Temps modernes*, **No. 434,** (September 1982), pp. 449–75.

98 J D Wilkinson, *The Intellectual Resistance in Europe* (Harvard University Press, 1981), p. 35.

99 Astruc and Contat, Sartre, pp. 66–7.

100 P Mignon, 'Le Théâtre de A à Z: Jean-Paul Sartre', in *L'Avant-scène théâtre*, Nos. 402–3 (1–15 May 1968) in M. Contat and M. Rybalka, (eds) Sartre: Un Théâtre de situations (Gallimard, 1973), p. 221. [Hereafter Sartre: Théâtre de situations]

101 For the full text of the play see Contat and Rybalka, *Écrits de Sartre*, pp. 565–633.

102 Beauvoir, *Céréremonie*, p. 237–8.

103 I Galster, *Le Théâtre de Jean-Paul Sartre devant ses premiers critiques* (Éditions Jean-Michel Place, 1986).

104 Beauvoir, *Cérémonie*, p. 492.

105 Ibid., p. 494.

106 Gerassi, op. cit., p. 175.

107a G. Chazelas, quoted in Cohen-Solal, *Sartre*, p. 242

107 Raoul Lévy, quoted in Cohen-Solal, *Sartre*, p. 243.

108 Raoul Lévy, quoted in Gerassi, op. cit., p. 178.

109 Dominique and Jean-Toussaint Desanti, quoted in Cohen-Solal, *Sartre*, p. 242.

110 Quoted in D Bair, *Simone de Beauvoir* (Jonathan Cape, 1990), **p. 254.**

111 'Ce que nous dit Jean-Paul Sartre de sa première pièce', interview with Yvon Novy, *Comœdia* (24 April 1943).

112 Sartre, 'Hommage à Jean Giraudoux', *Comœdia* (5 February 1944).

113 Sartre, 'Drieu la Rochelle ou la haine de soi', *Les Lettres françaises*, No. 6 (April 1943).

114 Ibid.

115 Sartre, 'La littérature, cette liberté', *Les Lettres françaises*, No. 15 (April 1944).

116 Ibid.

117 Sartre, 'L'Espoir fait l'homme', *Les Lettres françaises*, No. 18 (July 1944).

118 Ibid.

119 Sartre, 'Un film pour l'après-guerre', *Les Lettres françaises*, No. 15 (April 1944).

120 Ibid.

121 Sartre, *Lettres au Castor et à quelques autres*, Vol. 2 (Gallimard, 1983), p. 200.

122 Sartre, 'Explication of *L'Etranger*', *Cahiers du Sud*, No. 253 (February 1943). A Camus, Review of *Le Mur*, *Alger Républicain*, 12, (March 1939), A Camus, Review of *La Nausée*, *Alger Républicain*, 20 (October 1938)

123 'Ce que nous dit Jean-Paul Sartre de sa première pièce', op. cit.

124 Quoted in Sartre, *Théâtre de situations*, p. 236.

125 'Jean-Paul Sartre à Berlin: discussion autour des *Mouches*', *Verger* No. 5 (1948); quoted in Sartre, *Théâtre de situations*, pp. 230–31.

126 Ibid.

127 Quoted in Galster, op. cit., p. 62.

128 Sartre, 'Paris sous l'occupation', *La France libre*, No. 49 (15 November 1944); reproduced in Sartre, *Situations III* (Gallimard, 1949; new edition 1976), **pp. 15–42.**

129 Astruc and Contat, *Sartre*, p. 69.

130 Galster, '*Les Mouches* sous l'Occupation: à propos de quelques idées reçues', *Les Temps modernes*, Témoins de Sartre Vol 2 (October-December 1990), p. 850.

131 Galster, *Théâtre*, p. 179.

132 R Aronson, *Jean-Paul Sartre: Philosophy in the World* (New Left Books, 1980), p. 71.

133 Sartre, *L'Être et le néant*, (Gallimard, 1981), p. 34.

134 Sartre, 'La République du silence', *Les Lettres françaises*, No. 2 (9 September 1944); reproduced in Sartre, *Situations III*, p. 20.

135 *L' Existentialisme est un humanisme*, (Nagel, 1946), p. 17.

136 Aronson, op. cit., p. 84.

137 R. Kearney, *Modern Movements in European Philosophy* (Manchester University Press, 1986), p. 64.

138 Ibid., p. 68.

139 Spoken preface to a sound recording, *Deutsche Gramophon Gesellschaft* No. 43902/03; quoted in Contat and Rybalka, *Écrits de Sartre*, p. 101.

140 Ibid., pp. 103–106.

141 Bair, op. cit., p. 293

142 H. Lottman, *The Left Bank, Writers in Paris from Popular Front to Cold War*, (Heinemann, 1982), p. 193.

143 *Action* (29 September 1944); *Ce Soir* (14 November 1944), quoted in Galster, op. cit., pp. 278–79.

144 Astruc and Contat, *Sartre*, p. 70.

145 Beauvoir, *La Force des choses*, p. 13.

146 Sartre, 'Quand Hollywood veut faire penser . . . *Citizen Kane* d'Orson Welles', *L'Écran français*, No. 5 (1 August 1945).

147 Sartre, 'Le Président Roosevelt dit aux journalistes Français son amour de notre pays', *Le Figaro* (11–12 March 1945); quoted in Contat and Rybalka, *Écrits de Sartre*, p. 119.

148 Beauvoir, *La Force des Choses*, p. 50.

149 Sartre, 'La Nationalisation de la Littérature,' *Les Temps modernes*, No. 2 (November 1945), pp. 193–211, reproduced in Sartre, *Situations II* (Gallimard, 1948), p. 43.

150 Gavi et al, *On a raison*, p. 26.

151 Sartre, 'A propos de l'existentialisme: Mise au point', *Action*, No. 17 (29 December 1944). See Contat and Rybalka, *Écrits de Sartre*, p. 653–8.

152 Gavi et al., *On a raison*, p. 26.

153 Sartre, *Letttres au Castor*, vol. 2, p. 333.

154 Ibid., p. 334.

155 Beauvoir, *Force des choses*, p. 82.

156 Interview with J Gerassi, Sartre, *Œuvres romanesques*, p. lxiv.

157 Sartre, 'Matérialisme et révolution', *Les Temps modernes*, No.9 (June 1946).

158 *Les Temps modernes*, No.10 (July 1946). Both parts reproduced in Sartre, *Situations III*, pp. 135–225.

159 Sartre, *Refléxions sur la question juive* (Paul Morihien, 1946).

160 Sartre, 'Portrait de l'antisémite', *Les Temps modernes*, No. 3 (December 1945).

161 Sartre, 'Au procès des amis du Stern: Le problème juif? Un problème international, déclare Jean-Paul Sartre', *Franc-Tireur* (14 February 1948).

162 N Lamouchi, *Jean-Paul Sartre et le tiers monde*, (L'Harmattan, 1996), p 151.

163 Sartre, *Baudelaire* (Gallimard, 1963), p. 245.

164 Contat and Rybalka, *Écrits de Sartre*, p. 143.

165 Sartre, 'Qu'est-ce que la littérature?', *Les Temps modernes* (17 February 1947–22 July 1947); reproduced in Sartre, *Situations II*, p. 55–330.

166 Sartre, 'La Nationalisation de la littérature', pp. 33–53.

167 Sartre, 'Qu'est-ce que la Littérature?', pp. 277–8.

168 Ibid., p. 276.

169 Ibid., p. 277.

170 Ibid., p. 280.

171 Ibid.

172 Ibid., p. 287.

173 H Lefebvre, *L'Existentialisme* (Editions du Sagittaire, Paris, 1946).

174 Sartre, 'Le Cas Nizan', *Les Temps modernes*, No. 22 (July 1947).

175 Sartre, Preface to P. Nizan, *Aden Arabie*, p. 7.

176 *Carrefour* (29 October 1947); quoted in Contat and Rybalka, *Écrits de Sartre*, pp. 170–71.

177 Beauvoir, *Cérémonie*, p. 354.

178 R Aron, *Mémoires*, p.317.

179 Sartre, 'Appel du comité pour le Rassemblement démocratique révolutionnaire', in Contat and Rybalka, *Écrits de Sartre*, p. 197.

180 Ibid.

181 Sartre, 'Le RDR et le problème de la liberte', *La Pensée socialiste*, No. 19 (1948).

182 Gavi et al, *On a raison*, p. 29.

183 Ibid., pp. 28–9.

184 Sartre et al, *Entretiens sur la politique* (Gallimard, 1949).

185 D Rousset, 'Sartre et la politique', *Études sociales, politiques, économiques*, No. 406 (28 April 1980), p. 3.

186 Sartre, Interview in *Franc-Tireur* (25 March 1948); reproduced in Contat and Rybalka, *Sartre: Théâtre de situations*, p. 246.

187 Sartre, Interview in *Combat* (31 March 1948); reproduced in Contat and Rybalka, *Sartre: Théâtre de situations*, p. 247.

188 Sartre, Interview with Paolo Caruso (1964) in Contat and Rybalka, *Sartre: Théâtre de situations*, p. 249.

189 F Erval, 'Jean-Paul Sartre reproche à Georges Lukács de ne pas être marxiste', *Combat* (20 January 1949).

190 Sartre, *Cahiers pour une morale* (Gallimard, 1983).

191 Margarete Buber-Neumann, *Milena* (London, 1990), p. 7.

192 Sartre and M Merleau-Ponty, 'Les Jours de notre vie'; R Stéphane, 'La Question du travail forcé á l'ONU', *Les Temps modernes*, No. 51, (January 1950).

193 Sartre, 'Faux Savants ou faux lièvres', preface to L. Delmas, *Le Communisme yougoslave*; reproduced in Sartre, *Situations VI* (Gallimard, 1964), pp. 23–68.

194 Quoted in Contat and Rybalka, *Écrits de Sartre*, p. 223.

195a Sartre, 'Merleau-Ponty Vivait', *Les Temps Modernes Situations IV*, p. 248

195 Sartre, 'Merleau-Ponty', in Sartre, *Situations IV*, p. 238.

196 Ibid., pp. 239–40.

197 Ibid., p. 239.

198 Ibid., p. 237.

199 Interview in *Samedi soir* (2 June 1951); reproduced in Sartre, *Théâtre de situations*, pp. 268–9.

200 Sartre, 'The Chances of Peace', *The Nation* (30 December 1950).

201 'Et Bourreaux et victimes . . .', *Les Temps modernes*, No. 15 (December 1946).

202 Sartre, *L'Affaire Henri Martin* (Gallimard, 1953).

203 F Giles, *The Locust Years: The Story of the Fourth French Republic 1946–1958*, (Secker & Warburg, 1990), p. 164.

204 Astruc and Contat, *Sartre*, pp. 91–2.

205 Sartre, 'Merleau-Ponty', pp. 248–9.

206 Sartre, 'Les Communistes et la paix', Part 1, *Les Temps modernes*, No.81 (July 1952). For the whole text (Parts 1–3), see *Situations VI*, pp. 80–384.

207 Sartre, 'Les Communistes et la paix', p. 168.

208 Sartre, 'Les Communistes et la paix', Part 2, *Les Temps modernes*, Nos. 84–5 (October–November 1952).

209 F Jeanson, 'Albert Camus ou l'âme révolté', *Les Temps modernes*, No. 79 (May 1952).

210 A Camus, Lettre au directeur des *Temps modernes*, *Les Temps modernes* No. 82 (August 1952).

211 Sartre, 'Réponse à Albert Camus', *Les Temps modernes*, No. 82 (August 1952); reproduced in Sartre, *Situations IV*, pp. 90–125.

212 Sartre, *Saint Genet* (Gallimard, 1952).

213 Ibid., p. 549.

214 Sartre, 'Ce que j'ai vu à Vienne, c'est la Paix', *Les Lettres françaises* (1–8 January 1953); extract quoted in Contat and Rybalka, *Écrits de Sartre*, p. 255.

215 Sartre, 'Réponse à Claude Lefort', *Les Temps modernes*, No. 89 (April 1953); reproduced in *Situations VII*, (Gallimard, 1965), pp. 7–93.

216 Text of speech reproduced in *Défense de la paix* (June 1953), see Contat and Rybalka, *Écrits de Sartre*, p. 265.

217 Manuscript quoted in Cohen-Solal, *Sartre*, p. 465.

218 Astruc and Contat, *Sartre*, pp. 110–12.

219 Sartre, 'Les Animaux malades de la rage', *Libération* (22 June 1953); text reproduced in Contat and Rybalka, *Écrits de Sartre*, pp. 704–8.

220 *Les Temps modernes*, No. 92 (July 1953).

221 Sartre, Interview in *Combat* (5 November 1953), see *Sartre: Théâtre de Situations*, p. 284.

222 J Cau, *Croquis de mémoire* (Paris, 1985), p. 114.

223 Beauvoir, *Cérémonie*, p. 421.

224 Ibid., p. 424.

225 Ibid., p. 462.

226 Sartre, *Libération* (20 July 1954).

227 *France-URSS*, No. 107 (August 1954), No. 108 (September 1954).

228 Sartre, ;Autoportrait à soixante-dix ans, p. 220.

229 Interview in *L'Humanité* (8 June 1955), see Sartre: *Théâtre de Situations*, p. 294.

230 Interview in *Combat* (7 June 1955), see Sartre: *Théâtre de situations*, p. 292.

231 See Contat and Rybalka, *Écrits de Sartre*, p. 256.

232 *L'Humanité* (8 June 1955), in Sartre: *Théâtre de situations*, p. 294.

233 De Beauvoir, quoted in Bair, *Simone de Beauvoir* (Jonathan Cape, 1990), p. 462–3.

234 Sartre, 'La Chine que j'ai vue', *France-Observateur* (1, 8 December 1955), in Contat and Rybalka, *Les Écrits de Sartre*, p. 292–293.

235 Sartre, 'Le Colonialisme est un système', *Les Temps modernes*, No. 123 (March–April 1956); reproduced in *Situations V*, (Gallimard, 1964), pp. 25–48.

236 'Le Réformisme et les fétiches' *Les Temps Modernes*, No. 122, February 1956, reproduced in Sartre, *Situations VII*, p. 117.

237 Ibid., p. 110.

238 Bair, op. cit., p. 462.

239 Sartre, 'Après Budapest', *L'Express*, No. 281 (9 November 1956); see Contat and Rybalka, *Les Écrits de Sartre*, p. 305.

240 Ibid., pp. 305–6.

241a Ibid., p. 306.

241 Sartre, 'Le Fantôme de Staline', *Les Temps modernes*, Nos. 129–31 (November–December 1956; January 1957), pp. 577–697; reproduced in Sartre, *Situations VII*, pp. 144–307.

242 Sartre, 'Questions de méthode', *Les Temps modernes*, Nos. 139–40 (September–October 1957), pp. 761–800. Published in book form by Gallimard, (1960).

243 Sartre, 'Questions de méthode', pp. 11–12.
244 Ibid., p. 12.
245 Ibid., p. 14.
246 Ibid., p. 41.
247 Preface to A Memmi, *Portrait du colonisé*, preceded by *Portrait du colonisateur* (Corrêa, 1957). Published in *Les Temps modernes*, No. 137–8 (July–August 1957), pp. 289–93. Reproduced in Sartre, *Situations V*, pp. 49–56.
248 *Cérémonie*, pp. 417–18.
249 Sartre, 'Le Prétendant', *L'Express* (22 May 1958); reproduced in *Situations V*, pp. 89–101.
250 Sartre, 'La Constitution du mépris', *L'Express* (11 September 1958); reproduced in *Situations V*, pp. 102–112.
251 Sartre, 'Autoportrait à soixante-dix ans', p. 150.
252 'Interview de Sartre', *Vérités pour . . .* (2 June 1959), pp. 14–17, see Contat and Rybalka, *Les Écrits de Sartre*, pp. 723–9.
253 Sartre, *Lettres au Castor*, Vol 2, p. 360.
254 See R Aronson, *Sartre and Camus: The Story of a Friendship and the Quarrel that Ended It* (University of Chicago Press, 2004).
255 See D Drake, 'Sartre, Camus and the Algerian War', *Sartre Studies International*, Volume 5, No. 1 (1999), pp.16–32.
256 Sartre, 'Albert Camus', *France-Observateur*, No. 505 (7 January 1960); reproduced in Sartre, *Situations IV*, pp. 126–129.
257 Contat and Rybalka, *Écrits de Sartre*, p. 339.
258 Sartre, *Critique de la raison dialectique* (Gallimard, 1985), p. 406.
259 'Une Vie pour la philosophie: entretien avec Jean-Paul Sartre', *Magazine littéraire*, No. 384 (February 2000), p. 44; interview conducted in 1975.
260 Ibid.
261 Sartre, *Critique de la raison dialectique*, Vol II: *L'Intelligibilité de l'histoire* (Gallimard, 1985).
262 Sartre, 'Idéologie et révolution', *Obliques*, No. 18–19 (Paris, 1979), p. 297.
263 'Ouragon sur le sucre: Un grand reportage à Cuba de Jean-Paul Sartre sur Fidel Castro', *France-Soir* (28 June–15 July 1960).
264 'Jeuness et guerre d'Algérie', *Vérité-Liberté*, No. 3 (July–August 1960).
265 'L'Assaut contre Castro', *L'Express* (20 April 1961).
266 'Merleau-Ponty vivant', *Les Temps modernes*, Nos. 183–85 (October 1961), pp. 304–76; reprinted in Sartre *Situations IV*, pp. 189–287.
267 Sartre, 'Préface' to F Fanon, *Les Damnés de la Terre* (Maspero, 1961).
268 Sartre and B Lévy, *L'Espoir maintenant* (Verdier, 1991), p. 65.
269 Sartre, Forword to P Nizan, *Aden Arabie*; reproduced in Sartre, *Situations IV*, p. 138.
270 Quoted in M-A Burnier, *Les Existentialistes et la politique* (Gallimard, 1966), p. 145.
271 Sartre, 'Le Démilitarisation de la culture', *Situations VII*, p. 331.
272 See E Bérard-Zarzycka, 'Sartre et de Beauvoir en URSS', *Commentaire*, No. 53 (Spring 1991), pp. 161–68.
273 Sartre, 'La Pensée politique de Patrice Lumumba', *Situations V*, pp. 194–253.
274 Contat and Rybalka, *Écrits de Sartre*, p. 389.
275 *Les Temps modernes*, No. 209 (October 1963), pp. 577–649; No. 210 (November 1963), pp. 769–834.
276 'Jean-Paul Sartre s'explique sur *Les Mots*, *Le Monde* 18 April 1964, see Contat & Rybalka, *Écrits de Sartre*, p. 385.
277 Astruc & Contat, *Sartre*, p. 111.
278 'Jean-Paul Sartre s'explique.', p. 386.
279 Astruc & Contat, *Sartre*, p. 111.
280 Beauvoir, *Cérémonie*, p. 275.
281 Quoted in Cohen-Solal, p. 570.

282 Quoted in M. Contat, 'Rien dans les mains, rien dans les poches', *Quai Voltaire*, No. 6 (Autumn 1992), p. 86.

283 Sartre: *Un Théâtre de situations*, p. 364.

284 Contat, 'Rien dans les mains . . .', p. 87.

285 Ibid.

286 Sartre, 'Plaidoyer pour les intellectuels', *Situations VIII*, (Gallimard, 1972), pp. 375–455.

287 Sartre, 'Sartre à de Gaulle', *Le Nouvel Observateur* (26 April 1967), in Sartre, *Situations VIII*, p. 47.

288 Published in *Le Monde* (1 June 1967); see Contat and Rybalka, *Écrits de Sartre*, p. 444.

289 *Les Temps modernes*, No. 253 bis (June 1967).

290 'Jean-Paul Sartre répond', *L'Arc*, No. 30 (1966), pp. 87–8.

291 *Le Monde* (15 March 1968).

292 *Le Monde* (8 May 1968).

293 'Il est capital que le mouvement des étudiants oppose et maintienne une puissance de refus, déclarent MM Jean-Paul Sartre, Henri Lefebvre et un groupe d'écrivains et de philosophes', *Le Monde* (10 May 1968).

294 Quoted in Contat and Rybalka, *Écrits de Sartre*, pp. 463–4.

295 'L'Imagination au pouvoir'; special supplement to *Le Nouvel Observateur* (20 May 1968); reproduced in J Sauvegeot et al., *La Révolution étudiante: les animateurs parlent* (Éditions du Seuil, 1968), pp. 86–97.

296 'M. Jean-Paul Sartre à la Sorbonne: pour l'association du socialisme et de la liberté', *Le Monde* (22 May 1968); 'Sartre à la Sorbonne en mai 1968', *Le Nouvel Observateur* (27 May–2 June 1988).

297 Sartre, 'Les Bastilles de Raymond Aron', *Le Nouvel Observateur* (15–19 June 1968); reproduced in Sartre, *Situations VIII*, pp. 175–192.

298 Sartre, 'L'Idée neuve de mai 1968', *Le Nouvel Observateur* (26 June 1968); reproduced in Sartre, *Situations VIII*, pp. 193–194.

299 Gavi et al., *On a raison*, p. 63.

300 'M J-P Sartre: le parti communiste a trahi la revolution de mai', *Le Monde* (16 July 1968).

301 Sartre, 'Itinerary of a Thought', in Sartre, *Between Existentialism and Marxism* (New Left Books, 1974), p. 60.

302 Interview in *Paese Sera* (25 August 1968).

303 Sartre, short declaration to *Svobodne Slovo* (29–30 November 1968); see Contat and Rybalka, *Écrits de Sartre*, p. 473.

304 Quoted in Cohen-Solal, *Sartre*, p. 592.

305 *Le Figaro* (28 May 1970).

306 Sartre, 'Plaidoyer pour les intellectuels', in Sartre, *Situations VIII* (Gallimard, 1972), p. 426.

307 Gavi et al, *On a raison . . .*, p. 77.

308 *Le Monde* (10 March 1972); quoted in J-P Boulé, *Sartre médiatique* (Librairie Minard, 1992), p. 126.

309 Gavi, *On a raison*

310 Sartre, 'Itinerary of a Thought'.

311 Ibid., p. 43.

312 Astruc and Contat, *Sartre*, p. 130.

313 Sartre, *Carnets*, p. 197; emphasis in original.

314 Interview with Michel Sicard, *Obliques*, Nos. 18–19 (1979), p. 18.

315 F Sagan, *Avec mon meilleur souvenir* (Paris, 1984); quoted in W Bourton, *Sartre, d'un siècle l'autre* (Éditions Labor, 2005), p. 96.

316 For more on this episode, see M Scriven, *Sartre and the Media* (London: St Martin's Press, 1993), pp. 98–114.

317 *Obliques*, p. 14.

318 Ibid., p. 16.

319 Cohen-Solal, *Sartre*, p. 634.

320 Sartre, *Œuvres romanesques*, p. ci.

321 E Said, 'My Encounter with Sartre', *London Review of Books*, No. 11 (1 June 2000).

322 Ibid.

323 De Beauvoir, *Cérémonie*, p. 150.

Chronology

Year	Date	Life
1905	21 June	Birth in Paris of Jean-Paul-Charles-Eymard Sartre.
1906	17 September	15 months. Death of Jean-Baptiste Sartre. (Sartre's father). Mother and Jean-Paul move in with her parents in Meudon.
1908	9 January	2 years 7 months. Birth of Simone de Beauvoir.
1909		Loses most of his sight in his right eye.
1911		Schweitzer/Sartre family moves to Paris.
1917	November	Sartre's mother marries Joseph Mancy. Father moves to La Rochelle.

Year	History	Culture
1905	Demonstrations in St. Petersburg brutally crushed; first workers' soviet formed; Czar Nicholas II promises reforms.	Cezanne, *Les Grandes Baigneuses*. R. Strauss, *Salome*. A. Einstein, *Special Theory of Relativity*.
1906	France and Spain assume control of Morocco. Alfred Dreyfus rehabilitated.	M. Gorky, *The Mother*. H. Matisse, *Bombeur de vivre*. P.G. Wodehouse, *Love Among the Chickens*.
1908	Young Turks revolt in Resina. Union of South Africa established. Crete proclaims union with Greece.	E. M. Forster, *A Room with a View*. G. Mahler, *Das Lied von der Erde* (until 1909). Cubism begins.
1909	Turkey and Serbia recognize Austria's annexation of Bosnia and Herzegovina.	Rabindranath Tagore, *Gitanjali*. Sergey Diaghilev forms Les Ballets Russes. F. T. Marinetti publishes manifesto of Futurism in *Le Figaro*.
1911	Arrival of German gunboat in Agadir creates international crisis; Kaiser asserts Germany's 'Place in the Sun'.	Renoir, *Gabrielle with a Rose*. Braque, *Man with a Guitar*. Matisse, *Red Studio*. R. Strauss, *Der Rosenkavalier*
1917	Pétain becomes French Commander-in-Chief; Pershing arrives in Paris to head US forces. October Revolution in Russia.	G. de Chirico, *Le Grand Metaphysique*. Gershwin, *Rialto Ripples*. First recording of New Orleans jazz.

Year	Date	Life
1920	Autumn	Sartre returns to Paris. He is a boarder at Henri-IV.
1922	Summer	Writes 'L'Ange du morbide' and *Jésus la chouette*.
	Autumn	Moves (as does Nizan) to the Lycée Louis-le-Grand.
1923		Publishes 'L'Ange du morbide' and chapters of *Jésus la chouette* in *La Revue sans titre*.
1924		Enrols at the *École Normale Supérieure* (ENS).
1928	July	Sartre fails the final year examination (*l'agrégation*).
1929	July	Meets Simone de Beauvoir. Comes first in the *agrégation* (Beauvoir comes second).
	November	Begins military service at Saint-Cyr.
1930		Death of maternal grandmother. Sartre receives inheritance of around 100,000 francs.
1931		End of military service. Teaching post in Le Havre; Beauvoir takes a teaching post in Marseilles. 'Légende de la vévrité' published in *Bifur*.

Year	History	Culture
1920	In Paris the League of Nations comes into being. 19th Amendment gives US women the right to vote.	C. Chaplin, *The Kid*. F. Kafka, *The Country Doctor*. E. Wharton, *The Age of Innocence*.
1922	Mussolini's March on Rome. Atatürk declared Turkey a republic. Irish Free State proclaimed.	J. Joyce, *Ulysses*. M. Yourcenar, *The God's are not Dead*.
1923	French Army occupies German cities of Darmstadt, Karlsruhe, and Mannheim.	Le. Corbusier, *Vers une architecture*.
1924	Lenin dies; Stalin outmaneuvers Trotsky in race for succession.	E. M. Forster, *A Passage to India*. G. Gershwin, *Rhapsody in Blue*.
1928	Kellogg-Briand Pact for Peace signed in Paris. Alexander Fleming discovers penicillin.	G. Gershwin, *An American in Paris*. D. H. Lawrence, *Lady Chatterley's Lover*. M. Ravel, *Bolero*.
1929	Lateran Treaty. Yugoslavia under kings of Serbia. Wall Street crash. Young Plan for Germany.	S. Dali, *The Great Masturbator*. E. Hemingway, *A Farewell to Arms*. S. Prokofiev, *The Prodigal Son*. M. Yourcenar, *Alexis*.
1930	M. Gandhi leads Salt March in India. Frank Whittle patents turbo-jet engine. Pluto discovered.	W. H. Auden, *Poems*. T. S. Eliot, *Ash Wednesday*. W. Faulkner, *As I Lay Dying*.
1931	Spanish republic formed. New Zealand becomes independent. Japan occupies Manchuria. Building of Empire State Building completed in New York.	S. Dali, *The Persistence of Memory*. M. Yourcenar, *The New Eurydice*.

Year	Date	Life
1933	September	Sartre receives a grant to study at the French Institute in Berlin where he replaces Aron. Aron takes Sartre's place at the *lycée* in Le Havre
1934		In Berlin, completes a second version of *La Nausée* and writes *La Transcendance de l'ego*.
	October	Resumes teaching in Le Havre.
1935	February	Experiments with mescaline.
	21 March	Death of Charles Schweitzer aged 91.
	Autumn	Olga Kosakiewicz starts to play an important part in lives of Sartre and Beauvoir.
1936		*L'Imagination* published. Consolidation of three-way relationship with Beauvoir and Olga. Gallimard publishing house turns down *La Nausée*.
	Autumn	Sartre takes up new teaching post at Laon, Beauvoir is appointed as a teacher at the Lycée Molière in Paris.
1937		Publication of *La Transcendance de l'ego*.
	Spring	Meets Wanda Kosakiewicz, sister of Olga.
	July	*Le Mur* published in the NRF française.
	Autumn	Appointed as teacher to the Lycée Pasteur in Neuilly.
1938		Publication of short stories 'La Chambre', 'Intimité' and 'Nourritures'.
	April	Publication of *La Nausée*.
	July	Completes 'L'Enfance d'un chef'.

Year	History	Culture
1933	Nazi Party wins German elections; A. Hitler appointed chancellor. F D Roosevelt president in US; launches New Deal.	B. Britten, *Sinfonietta*, A. Malraux, *La condition humaine*. G. Orwell, *Down and Out in Paris and London*. G. Stein, *The Autobiography of Alice B. Toklas*. P.G. Wodehouse, *Heavy Weather*.
1934	In Germany, the Night of the Long Knives. In China, the Long March. Enrico Fermi sets off first controlled nuclear reaction.	A. Christie, *Murder on the Orient Express*. H. Miller, *Tropic of Cancer*. G. Orwell, *Burmese Days*. D. Shostakovitch, *Lady Macbeth of Mtsensk*.
1935	In Germany, Nuremberg Laws enacted. Philippines becomes self-governing. Italy invades Ethiopia.	Marx Brothers, *A Night at the Opera*. G. Gershwin, *Porgy and Bess*. G. Orwell, *A Clergyman's Daughter*.
1936	Germany re-occupies Rhineland. Edward VIII abdicates throne in Britain; George VI becomes king. Spanish Civil War (until 1939).	L. Armstrong, *Swing that Music*. S. Prokofiev, *Peter and the Wolf*. O. Welles, 'voodoo' Macbeth. BBC public television founded.
1937	Arab-Jewish conflict in Palestine. Japan invades China. Nanjing massacre.	S. Dali, *Dream of Venus*. G. Orwell, *The Road to Wigan Pier*. Picasso, Guernica. J. Steinbeck, *Of Mice and Men*.
1938	Kristallnacht: in Germany, Synagogues are burnt down, and shops looted. Munich Crisis: Czechoslovakia cedes Sudetenland.	Greene, *Brighton Rock*. G. Orwell, *Homage to Catalonia*. P.G. Wodehouse, *The Code of the Woosters*. M. Yourcenar, *Dreams and Destinies*.

Year	Date	Life
1939	2 September	Called up as part of general mobilization.
1940	March	Publication of *L'Imaginaire*.
	April	On leave in Paris. Awarded Roman populaiste prize for *Le Mur*. (Published February 1939)
	21 June	Captured on 35th birthday. Held in Baccarat until mid-August and the transferred to POW camp Stalag 12 D in Trier (Trèves).
	24, 25, 26 December	*Bariona* staged in POW camp.
1941		Released from POW camp.
	April	Resumes teaching at the Lycée Pasteur. Founds 'Socialism and Freedom' resistance group.
	Summer	Bicycles with Beauvoir to south of France in abortive attempt to persuade André Gide and André Malraux to join 'Socialism and Freedom'. Begins writing *The Flies*.
	October	Appointed as a teacher at the Lycée Condorcet (Paris). Dissolves 'Socialism and Freedom' group.
	December	Begins writing *L'Être et le néant*.
1942	October	Completes *L'Être et le néant*.
1943		Joins the intellectual resistance group Comité national des écrivains (CNE)
	2 June	Première of *The Flies*. Meets Camus at the dress rehearsal.
	Summer	Publication of *L'Être et le néant*.
	Autumn	Writes *Huis clos*. Offers part of Garcin to Camus.

Year	History	Culture
1939	1 September: Germany invades Poland. Francisco Franco becomes dictator of Spain. Britain and France declare war on Germany.	J. Ford, *Stagecoach* with John Wayne. S. Dali, *The Secret Life of Salvador Dali*. Selznick, *Gone With the Wind*. Steinbeck, *Grapes of Wrath*.
1940	Germany occupies France, Belgium, the Netherlands, Norway and Denmark. In Britain, Winston Churchill becomes PM. Leon Trotsky assassinated in Mexico.	C. Chaplin, *The Great Dictator*. Disney, Fantasia. E. Hemingway, *For Whom the Bell Tolls*. S. Prokofiev, *Romeo and Juliet*.
1941	Operation Barbarossa: Germany invades Soviet Union. Japan attacks Pearl Harbour: US enter Second World War. B.	Brecht, Mother *Courage and Her Children*. S. Dali, *Hidden Faces*. B. Britten, *Paul Bunyan*. O. Welles, *Citizen Kane*.
1942	US troops land in French North Africa; French navy scuttled in Toulon.	A. Camus, *L'Etranger*. Rakhmaninov dies. Rodgers and Hammerstein, *Oklahoma!*
1943	Allies bomb Germany. Allies invade Italy: Mussolini deposed. Albert Hoffman discovers hallucinogenic properties of LSD.	T. S. Eliot, *Four Quartets*. R. Rodgers and O. Hammerstein, *Oklahoma*. Sartre, *Being and Nothingness*. *Casablanca* with Ingrid Bergman and Humphrey Bogart.

Year	Date	Life
1944	27 May	Premiere of *Huis clos*.
	August – September	Articles under Sartre's name on the Liberation of Paris appear in *Combat*.
1945		Refuses the Légion d'honneur.
	12 January	Flies to USA where he meets Dolorès Vannetti, with whom he has affair. Also meets President Roosevelt and Henriette Nizan.
	21 January	Death aged 70 of step-father, Joseph Mancy.
	Autumn	'Existentialist offensive' (Beauvoir).
	15 October	First issue of *Les Temps modernes*.
	29 October	Gives public lecture on existentialism at the Club Maintenant.
1946	March	Publication of *L'Existentialisme est un humanisme*.
	October	Moves with his mother into a flat, 42 rue Bonaparte.
1947		Publication of *Baudelaire*.
	October–November	Series of nine radio programmes *La Tribune des Temps modernes* of which six were broadcast.
1948	February	Joins the Rassemblement démocratique révolutionnaire (RDR).
	2 April	Premiere of *Dirty Hands*.
	May	Declaration of support for the creation of the state of Israel.
	October	All Sartre's works placed on Index by Vatican.
1949	12 October	Resigns from RDR.

Year	History	Culture
1944	Allies land in Normandy: Paris is liberated. Civil war in Greece.	J. L. Borges, *Fictions*. Eisenstein, *Ivan the Terrible*.
1945	8 May: Germany surrenders. United Nations formed. Atomic bombs dropped on Hiroshima and Nagasaki. 2 September: Japan surrenders.	B. Britten, *Peter Grimes*. G. Orwell, *Animal Farm*. K. Popper, *The Open Society and Its Enemies*.
1946	In Argentina, Juan Perón becomes president. In Britain, National Health Service founded. Winston Churchill makes 'Iron Curtain' speech.	Cocteau, *La belle et la bete*. S. Dali, *Madonna of Port Lligat*. B. Britten, *The Rape of Lucretia*. B. Russell, *Existentialism and Humanism*.
1947	Truman Doctrine. India becomes independent. Chuck Yeager breaks the sounds barrier.	B. Britten, *Albert Herring*. A. Frank, *The Diary of Anne Frank* (posth.). T. Williams, *A Streetcar Named Desire*.
1948	Marshall plan (until 1951). Soviet blockade of Western sectors of Berlin: US and Britain organize airlift. In South Africa, Apartheid legislation passed. Gandhi is assassinated. State of Israel founded.	B. Brecht, *Caucasian Chalk Circle*. B. Britten, *Saint Nicolas*. Greene, *The Heart of the Matter*. N. Mailer, *The Naked and the Dead*. A. Paton, *Cry, the Beloved Country*.
1949	NATO formed. Republic of Ireland formed. Mao proclaims China a People's Republic.	B. Britten, *The Spring Symphony*. A. Miller, *Death of a Salesman*. G. Orwell, *Nineteen Eighty-four*. O. Welles, *The Third Man*.

Year	Date	Life
1950	January	Editorial in *Les Temps modernes* signed by Sartre and Merleau-Ponty denouncing Soviet camps.
1951	7 June	Premiere of *Le Diable et le Bon Dieu*.
1952	January	Joins Communist campaign to free anti-war militant Henri Martin.
	August	Break with Albert Camus.
	12 December	Speech at international peace congress in Vienna.
1954	26 May–23 June	First trip to the USSR.
	July	49. Publication of controversial series of interviews about his trip to the USSR.
1955	8 June	Premiere of *Nekrassov*.
	26 June	50. Speech at international peace congress in Helsinki.
	September–November	Two months in China with Beauvoir. Meets Mao Zedong. Returns to France via USSR.

Year	History	Culture
1950	Schuman Plan. Korean War begins. China conquers Tibet. Stereophonic sound invented. First successful kidney transplant.	E. Ionesco, *The Bald Prima Donna*. Neruda, *Canto General*. Billy Wilder, *Sunset Boulevard*.
1951	Anzus pact in Pacific. German chancellor Adenauer visits Paris, Rome and London. Pétain dies.	B. Britten, *Billy Budd*. J. D. Salinger, *The Catcher in the Rye*. Stravinsky, *The Rake's Progress*. P.G. Wodehouse, *The Old Reliable*. M. Yourcenar, *Memoirs of Hadrian*.
1952	Gamal Abdel Nasser leads coup in Egypt. European Coal and Steel Community formed; Britain refuses to join. US tests hydrogen bomb. Elisabeth II becomes queen of Britain. McCarthy era begins in US.	S. Beckett, *Waiting for Godot*. E. Hemingway, *The Old Man and the Sea*. M. Tippett, *The Midsummer Marriage*. O. Welles, *Othello*. P.G. Wodehouse, *Barmy in Wonderland*. Chagall, *The Green Night*. Pollock, *Number 12*. Hepworth, Statue.
1954	Insurrection in Algeria. French withdrawal from Indochina: Ho Chi Minh forms government in North Vietnam.	B. Britten, *The Turn of the Screw*. 'The Seven Samurai' (Jap. film directed by Kurosawa). M. Ernst, *Lonely*. Matisse dies.
1955	West Germany joins NATO. Warsaw Pact formed.	O. Welles, *Mr. Arkadin* (*Confidential Report*). Picasso exhibition in Paris. Dali, *The Lord's Supper*.

Year	Date	Life
1956	27 January	Speech at a meeting in Paris denouncing colonialism in Algeria. Meets Arlette El Kaïm.
	9 November	Publication of interview condemning Soviet invasion of Hungary.
	November	Resigns from Franco-Soviet Association. 'Le Fantôme de Staline' published in *Les Temps modernes* (November 1956–January 1957).
1957	September–October	'Questions de méthode' published in *Les Temps modernes*.
1958	Spring	Accepts offer from John Huston to write the scenario for a film on Sigmund Freud.
	22 May	Publishes anti-de Gaulle article in *L'Express*.
	28 May/ 1 June	Joins anti-de Gaulle demonstrations.
	September	Articles in *L'Express* calling for a no vote in the referendum.
1959	May	Gives interview to the clandestine pro-FLN paper run by Francis Jeanson.
	24 September	Premiere of *Les Séquestrés d'Altona*.
1960	7 January	Publishes tribute to Camus in *France-Observateur*.
	22 February–20 March	Visits Cuba. Meets Fidel Castro, 'Che' Guevara and other leaders of the revolution.
	March	Completes the foreword to a new edition of Nizan's *Aden Arabie* (published in 1960).
	May	Visits Yugoslavia with Beauvoir. Meets Tito.
	August	Signs petition supporting those who refused to fight in Algeria.

Year	History	Culture
1956	Nikita Khruschev denounces Stalin. Suez Crisis. Revolts in Poland and Hungary. Fidel Castro and Ernesto 'Che' Guevara land in Cuba.	L. Armstrong, *Mack the Knife*. P.G. Wodehouse, *French Leave 1956*. M. Yourcenar, *The Alms of Alcippus and other poems*. Osborne, *Look Back in Anger*. Lampedusa, *The Leopard*. Bernstein, *Candide*.
1957	Treaty of Rome: EEC formed. USSR launches Sputnik 1. Ghana becomes independent.	B. Britten, *The Prince of the Pagodas*. Bernstein, *West Side Story*. O'Neill, *Long Day's Journey into Night* (posth.).
1958	Fifth French Republic; Charles De Gaulle becomes president. Great Leap Forward launched in China (until 1960). Castro leads communist revolution in Cuba.	Capote, *Breakfast at Tiffany's*. Pasternak, *Dr. Zhivago*. Guggenheim Museum, New York, designed by Frank Lloyd Wright, opens.
1959	In US, Alaska and Hawaii are admitted to the union. Solomon Bandaranaike, PM of Ceylon (Sri Lanka), is assassinated.	Grass, *Die Blechtrommel*. Miró: murals for UNESCO building, Paris. 'La Dolce Vita' (film directed by Fellini). 'Ben Hur' (film directed by B. Wilder wins Oscar)
1960	Vietnam War begins (until 1975). OPEC formed. Oral contraceptives marketed.	B. Britten, *A Midsummer Night's Dream*. P.G. Wodehouse, *Jeeves in the Offing*.

Year	Date	Life
1961	19 July	Sartre's flat bombed by the OAS (right-wing pro-French Algeria terrorist organization).
	November–December	Joins demonstrations on Algeria. Joins an anti-OAS demonstration.
1962	7 January	Second bomb attack on Sartre's flat.
	14 March	Elected vice-president of COMES, an organization bringing together writers from East and West.
	1–24 June	Visits USSR. Embarks on affair with guide and translator Léna Zonina.
1963	July	Essay on Patrice Lumumba published in *Présence africaine*.
	August–September	Attends COMES Congress in Leningrad.
	9 August	Meets Kruschev in Georgia.
	October–November	*Les Mots* serialized in *Les Temps modernes*.
	12–14 November	Visits Czechoslovakia with Beauvoir.
1964		Publication of *Situations IV, V, VI*.
	January	Les Mots published in book form.
	1 June–10 July	Visits Kiev, Leningrad, Moscow, Estonia
	22 October	Sartre awarded Nobel Prize for Literature (which he refuses).
	19 November	Gives an interview for the first issue of *Le Nouvel Observateur*.
1965		Publication of *Situations VII*.
	10 March	Premiere of *Les Troyennes*.
	18 March	Adopts Arlette El Kaïm as his daughter.
	March	Refuses to go to on lecture tour to the USA in protest at American involvement in Vietnam.
	July	Trip to USSR.
	13–14 July	Peace Conference in Helsinki calls for immediate withdrawal of US troops from Vietnam.
	December	Qualified support for François Mitterrand's candidature in presidential elections.

Year	History	Culture
1961	Berlin Wall erected. Bay of Pigs invasion. Yuri Gagarin is first man in space.	B. Britten, Cello Symphony. The Rolling Stones are formed. Rudolf Nureyev defects from USSR.
1962	Cuban missile crisis. Satellite television launched.	M. Yourcenar, *the Dark Brain of Piranesi*. Edward Albee, *Who's Afraid of Virginia Woolf?* David Lean directs 'Lawrence of Arabia'
1963	J. F. Kennedy assassinated; Martin Luther King leads March on Washington. Organisation of African Unity formed.	Betty Friedan, *The Feminine Mystique*. The Beatles, 'She Loves You'. 'Cleopatra' (Richard Burton and Elizabeth Taylor). Luchino Visconti directs 'The Leopard'.
1964	Kruschev ousted by Leonid Brezhnev. First race relations act in Britain. Civil Rights Act in US. PLO formed.	Harnick (lyrics) and Bock (music) *Fiddler on the Roof*. Saul Bellow, *Herzog*. Stanley Kubrick directs 'Doctor Strangelove'.
1965	Military coup in Indonesia.	Neil Simon, *The Odd Couple*.

Year	Date	Life
1966	2 May–6 June	Visits USSR. Alexander Solzhenitsyn refuses to meet him.
	July	Agrees to join Bertrand Russell's Tribunal on American war crimes in Vietnam.
1967	25 February–	Visit to Egypt.
	14–30 March	Visit to Israel.
	April	Corresponds with de Gaulle about Russell Tribunal.
	12 December	Death of Simone Jolivet.
1968	6 May	Supports student movement and denounces police repression.
	11 May	Interview on RTL.
	20 May	Sartre's interview with Daniel Cohn-Bendit published. Discusses with students in the occupied Sorbonne.
	24 August	Condemns Soviet intervention in Czechoslovakia.
	28 November–1 December	Visit to Czechoslovakia.
1969	30 January	Death of mother.
	10 February	Speaks at meeting protesting at expulsion of dissident university students. Turning point in his becoming a 'revolutionary intellectual'.
	March–April	Calls for no vote in referendum called by de Gaulle on regionalization.
1970	April	Agrees to become *directeur* – legally responsible for nominal editor of the Maoist newspaper *La Cause du peuple* (CDP). Beginning of Maoist phase and of friendship with Maoist leader, Pierre Victor (Benny Lévy).
	20, 26 June	Sells the CDP on streets of Paris. Arrested but immediately released.
	21 October	Addresses workers outside Renault factory.
	12 December	Heads a popular tribunal at Lens that finds bosses responsible for deaths of local miners.

Year	History	Culture
1966	France withdraws its troops from NATO. In the US, race riots.	John Lennon speculates that the The Beatles are more popular than Jesus. The band gives their last concert.
1967	Six day War between Israel and the Arab States. De Gaulle, on state visit to Canada, makes his 'free Quebec' peech. First heart transplant.	The Beatles, *Sergeant Pepper's Lonely Hearts Club Band*. Gabriel García Márquez, *One Hundred Years of Solitude*. Tom Stoppard, *Rosencrantz and Guildenstern are Dead*.
1968	Tet Offensive. In US, M L King and Robert Kennedy assassinated. In Paris, student riots.	Kubrick directs '2001: A Space Odyssey'. The Rollings Stones, *Beggar's Banquet*.
1969	Neil Armstrong takes first moon walk. Internet created by US Department of Defence. Massive anti-war rallies in US.	Mario Puzo, *The Godfather*. 'Easy Rider' (starring Dennis Hopper and Peter Fonda). 'Midnight Cowboy' becomes first wide-released X-rated film.
1970	Charles De Gaulle dies. Antonio Salazar dies. Gamel Abd el Nasser dies	Simon and Garfunkel *Bridge over troubled Water* Germaine Greer *The Female Eunuch*

Year	Date	Life
1971	13 February	Participates in illegal occupation of Sacré Cœur.
	April	Breaks with Cuba.
	May	Publication of first two volumes of *L'Idiot de la famille*.
	18 June	Founds the *Agence de Presse Libération* with novelist Maurice Clavel.
1972		Publication of *Situations VIII* and *IX* and of Vol 3 of *L'Idiot de la famille*.
	February–March	Autobiographical film *Sartre par lui-même* directed by A Astruc and M Contat.
	14 February	Forcibly ejected from inside Renault car factory where he had tried to hold a meeting.
	4 March	Joins march of 200,000 people protesting at the fatal shooting of a Maoist militant by a security guard at Renault.
	Winter	Active in preparing launch of new daily paper *Libération*.
1973	February	Denounces conditions under which members of Red Army Fraction (aka Baader-Meinhof gang) are held in prison.
	22 May	First issue of *Libération*.
	June	Loses sight in good eye.
	Summer	In Italy.
	Autumn	Pierre Victor/Benny Lévy become his secretary.
1974	May	Publication of conversations with Victor and Gavi as *On a raison de se révolter*.
	November	Plans television series on his take on the history of the twentieth century since his birth.
	4 December	Meets Andreas Baader in Stammheim Prison.
1976		Publication of *Situations X* and English translation of the *Critique de la raison dialectique*.
	27 October	Release of film *Sartre par lui-même*.
	7 November	Accepts honorary doctorate from Jerusalem University.

Year	History	Culture
1971	In Uganda, Idi Amin seizes power. Nixon proclaims end of US offensive role in Vietnam War.	Dmitri Shostakovich, *Symphony No. 15*. Solzhenitsyn, August 1914. Kubrick directs 'A Clockwork Orange'
1972	In US, Watergate scandal. Bloody Sunday massacre (N Ireland). Allende overthrown in Chile; Pinochet takes power. World Trade Centre completed. Optical fibre is invented.	Richard Adams, *Watership Down*. Bertolucci directs 'Last Tango in Paris'. Francis Ford Coppola directs 'The Godfather'.
1973	Yom Kippur War. Denmark, Ireland and Britain enter EC. US withdraws from Vietnam War. OPEC oil crisis.	Pink Floyd, *The Dark Side of the Moon*. Larkin, *High Windows*. E. F. Schumacher, *Small is Beautiful*. Truffaut, *Day for Night*.
1974	Watergate scandal; US President Richard Nixon forced to resign. Cyprus invaded by Turkey. Haile Selassie deposed in Ethiopia.	Dario Fo, *Can't Pay? Won't Pay!* Solzhenitsyn is expelled from the Soviet Union. Polanski (producer) 'Chinatown'.
1976	Argentina's President Perón overthrown by junta. North and South Vietnam reunited. US Bicentennial.	B. Britten, Phaedra. 'One Flew Over the Cuckoo's Nest' sweeps the board at the Oscars. Rev. Moon ends US ministry.

Year	Date	Life
1977		Publication of text of *Sartre par lui-même*.
	21 June	Attends reception for Russian dissidents held to coincide with official visit of Leonid Brezhnev.
	October–November	Denounces 'assassination' of Baader and his comrades.
1978	2–7 February	Visits Israel with Lévy and El Kaïm.
1979	15 March	Participates at an Arab-Israeli colloquium organized by Lévy.
	20 June	Participates at a press conference in favour of Vietnamese boat people. Meets Raymond Aron again.
	26 June	Received (with Aron) by President Giscard d'Estaing as part of campaign in favour of Vietnamese boat people.
1980	January	Protests at house arrest of Andrei Sakharov and calls for boycott of Moscow Olympics.
	March	Publication in *Le Nouvel Observateur* of dialogues with Lévy.
	20 March	Sartre hospitalized (Broussais Hospital).
	15 April	Dies at 9 p.m.
	19 April	Some 50,000 people line streets of Paris to pay final homage to Sartre. Buried in Montparnasse Cemetery.

Year	History	Culture
1977	Egyptian President Sadat arrives in Israel, first Arab leader to visit this country.	US space shuttle *Enterprise* makes its first manned flight. George Lucas directs 'Star Wars'.
1978		
1979	Shah of Iran is forced into exile. Idi Amin overthrown. Camp David Accords. Z. Bhutto hanged. M. Thatcher elected British PM.	P. Shaffer, *Amadeus*. Herbert Marcuse, Ger.-born Amer. philosopher and guru of sixties revolutionary movements, dies (b. 1898).
1980	A. Sakharov sent into exile in Gorki. US diplomats held hostage in Iran. Zimbabwe becomes independent. Lech Walesa becomes head of Polish trade union Solidarity.	M. Yourcenar, *With Open Eyes*. I. Murdoch, *Nuns and Soldiers*. Le Carré, *Smiley's People*. John Lennon is shot outside his New York apartment block. Hitchcock, Eng.-born Amer. film director, dies. Kokoschka, Austrian painter, dies.

Further Reading

Sartre in French

Dates refer to the publication in book form unless otherwise stated.
All titles published in Paris.

1936 *L'Imagination*
       La Transcendance de l'ego (in *Recherches philosophiques*, No. 6,
       1936–7, p. 85–123). Reissued in 1965.

1938 *La Nausée*

1939 *Le Mur* (contains 'Le Mur', 'L'Enfance d'un chef', 'Intimité',
       'La Chambre', 'Erostrate')
       Esquisse d'une théorie phénomenologique des émotions

1940 *L'Imaginaire*

1943 *Les Mouches*
       L'Être et le néant

1945 *Huis Clos*
       L'Age de raison
       Le Sursis

1946 *L'Existentialisme est un humanisme*
       Morts sans sépulture
       La Putain respectueuse
       Réflexions sur la question juive

1947 *Baudelaire*
       Situations I
       Les Jeux sont faits
       'Qu'est-ce que la littérature?' published in *Les Temps modernes*
       (February–July 1947)

1948 *Les Mains sales*

L'Engrenage

Situations II

1949 *La Mort dans l'âme*

Situations III

Entretiens sur la politique (with David Rousset and Gérard Rosenthal)

1951 *Le Diable et le Bon Dieu*

1952 *Saint Genet, comédien et martyr*

'Les Communistes et la paix', Parts 1 and 2 published in *Les Temps modernes* (July 1952, October–November 1952)

1953 *L'Affaire Henri Martin*

1954 'Les Communistes et la paix', Part 3 published in *Les Temps modernes* (April 1954)

1956 *Kean*

Nekrassov (first performed in 1955)

'Le Fantôme de Staline', published in *Les Temps modernes*

1958 'Questions de méthode' published in *Les Temps modernes*, (September, October 1957); later incorporated into the *Critique de la raison dialectique* (1960)

1959 *Les Séquestrés d'altona*

1960 *Critique de la raison dialectique*

1964 *Les Mots* (first published in *Les Temps modernes*, 1963)

Situations IV

Situations V

Situations VI

Situations VII

1966 *Les Troyennes* (first performed in 1965)

1970 *Écrits de Sartre* (ed. M Contat and M Rybalka). Contains, *inter alia*, the text of *Bariona*)

1971 *L'Idiot de la famille*, Vols 1 and 2

1972 *Situations VIII*

Situations IX

L'Idiot de la famille, Vol 3

1973 *Un Théâtre de situations* (ed. M Contat and M Rybalka).

1974 *On a raison de se révolter*

1976 *Situations X*

1977 *Sartre par lui-même* (transcript of film directed by A Astruc and M Contat)

Posthumous publications

1981 *Oeuvres romanesques* (ed. M Contat & M Rybalka)

1983 *Les Carnets de la drôle de guerre* (new expanded edition, 1995)
      Cahiers pour une morale
      Lettres au Castor et à quelques autres (2 volumes)

1984 *Le Scénario Freud* (ed. J B Pontalis)

1985 *Critique de la raison dialectique*, Volume Two

1986 *Mallarmé*

1989 *Vérité et existence*

1990 *Écrits de jeunesse*

1991 *La Reine Albermarle ou le dernier touriste*
      L'Espoir maintenant (with Benny Lévy)

Sartre in English

Fiction

The Age of Reason (*L'Âge de raison*), tr. Eric Sutton (New York and London, 1947)

The Reprieve (*Le Sursis*), tr. Eric Sutton (New York and London, 1947)

Nausea (*La Nausée*), tr. Robert Baldick (London, 1965). First published in English as *The Diary of Antoine Roquentin*, tr. Lloyd Alexander (New York and London, 1949)

Intimacy (*Le Mur*), tr. Lloyd Alexander (New York and London, 1949)

Iron in the Soul (*La Mort dans l'âme*), tr. Gerard Hopkins (London, 1950). Published in America as *Troubled Sleep* (New York, 1951)

Biography and autobiography

Baudelaire, tr. Martin Turnell (New York, 1950)

Saint Genet: Actor and Martyr, tr. Bernard Frechtman (New York, 1963)

The Words (*Les Mots*), tr. Bernard Frechtman (New York, 1964); *Words*, tr. Irene Clephane (London, 1964)

The Family Idiot (*Idiot de la famille*) Vol 1, tr. Carol Cosman (Chicago, 1981); Vol 2, tr. Carol Cosman (Chicago, 1987); Vol 3, tr. Carol Cosman (Chicago, 1989); Vol 4, tr. Carol Cosman (Chicago, 1991)

War Diaries (*Carnets de la drôle de guerre*), tr. Quentin Hoare, (London, 1984)

Mallarmé or the Poet of Nothingness, tr. Ernest Sturm (London and Pennsylvania State University Press, 1988)

Witness to My Life: The Letters of Jean-Paul Sartre to Simone de Beauvoir, 1926–1939, tr. Lee Fahnestock and Norman MacAfee (New York and Oxford, 1992)

Plays

The Flies (*Les Mouches*) and *In Camera* (*Huis Clos*), tr. Stuart Gilbert (London, 1946); *No Exit* (*Huis Clos*) (New York, 1947)

The Respectful Prostitute, tr. Kitty Black (London, 1947); tr. Lionel Abel (New York, 1949)

Men Without Shadows (*Morts sans sépulture*), tr. Kitty Black (London, 1947); *The Victors*, tr. Lionel Abel (New York, 1949)

Dirty Hands (*Les Mains sales*), tr. Kitty Black (London 1949); tr. Lionel Abel (New York, 1949)

Lucifer and the Lord (*le Diable et le Bon Dieu*), tr. Kitty Black (London, 1953); *The Devil and the Good Lord* (New York, 1960)

Kean or Disorder and Genius (*Kean*), tr. Kitty Black (London, 1954; New York, 1960)

Nekrassov, tr. Sylvia and George Leeson (Toronto 1957; London, 1958; New York, 1960)

Loser Wins (*Les Séquestrés d'Altona*), tr. Sylvia and George Leeson (London, 1960), *The Condemned of Altona*, (New York, 1961)

The Trojan Women (*Les Troyennes*), tr. Ronald Duncan (New York and London, 1967)

Screenplays

The Chips are Down (*Les Jeux sont faits*), tr. Louise Varèse (New York, 1948; London, 1951)

In the Mesh (*L'Engrenage*), tr. Mervyn Saville (London, 1954)

The Freud Scenario, tr. Quentin Hoare (London, 1985)

Philosophical Works

Existentialism (*L'Existentialisme est un humanisme*), tr. Bernard Frechtman (New York, 1947); *Existentialism and Humanism*, tr. Philip Mairet (London, 1948)

Outline of a Theory of the Emotions (*Esquisse d'une théorie des emotions*), tr. Bernard Frechtman (New York, 1948); *Sketch for a Theory of the Emotions*, tr. Philip Mairet (London, 1962)

Psychology of the Imagination (*L'Imaginaire*), tr. Bernard Frechtman (New York, 1948; London, 1948)

Imagination (*L'Imagination*), tr. Forrest Williams (New York, 1962)

Being and Nothingness (*L'Être et le néant*), tr. Hazel Barnes (New York, 1956; London, 1957)

The Transcendence of the Ego (*La Transcendance de l'ego*), tr. Forrest Williams and Robert Kirkpatrick (New York, 1957)

Search for a Method (*Questions de méthode*), tr. Hazel Barnes (New York, 1963); *The Problem of Method* (London, 1964)

Critique of Dialectical Reason (*Critique de la raison dialectique*), tr. Alan Sheridan Smith (London, 1976)

Hope Now (*L'Espoir maintenant*), tr. Adrian van den Hoven (Chicago and London, 1996)

Truth and Existence (*Vérité et existence*), tr. Adrian van den Hoven

(Chicago, 1992)

Notebook for an Ethics (*Cahiers pour une morale*), tr. David Pellauer (Chicago and London, 1992)

Essays

Anti-Semite and Jew (*Réflexions sur la question juive*), tr. George J. Becker (New York, 1948); *Portrait of an Anti-Semite*, tr. Eric de Mauny (London, 1948)

What is Literature? (*Qu'est-ce que la littérature?*), tr. Bernard Frechtman (New York, 1948)

Literary and Philosophical Essays, tr. Annette Michelson (New York and London, 1955)

Literary Essays, tr. Annette Michelson (New York, 1961)

Sartre on Cuba, (New York, 1961)

Essays in Aesthetics, tr. Wade Baskin (New York, 1963)

Situations (*Situations IV*), tr. Benita Eisler (New York, 1965)

The Communists and Peace with *A Reply to Claude Lefort* (*Les Communistes et la paix/Réponse à Claude Lefort*, published in *Situations VI*), tr. Martha H Fletcher with John R Kleinschmidt (New York, 1968)

The Spectre of Stalin (London, 1969)

Between Existentialism and Marxism (taken from *Situations VIII* and *Situations IX* with an interview 'Itinerary of a Thought' first published in *New Left Review*, No. 58), tr. John Matthews (London and New York, 1974)

Sartre on Theatre (*Un Théâtre de situations*), tr. Frank Jellinek (London and New York, 1976)

Sartre in the Seventies (*Situations X*), tr. Paul Auster and Lydia Davies (London, 1978)

Sartre by Himself (transcript of the film *Sartre par lui-même*), tr. Richard Seaver (New York, 1978)

Modern Times: *Selected Non-Fiction*, tr. Robin Buss, ed. Geoffrey Wall (London and New York, 2000)

Colonialism and Neocolonialism (*Situations V*), (London and New York, 2001)

Bibliographies

Contat, M and Rybalka M, *Les Écrits de Sartre* (Paris, 1970). English translation by Richard McCleary, *The Writings of Sartre*, 2 volumes, (Evanston, Illinois, 1974)

Contat and Rybalka's invaluable work stops in 1969 but various updates have been published elsewhere, notably:

Contat and Rybalka, 'Sartre 1969–1970: Bibliographie commentée', *Adam*, Nos. 343–5, 1970, p. 89–95

——————, 'Les Écrits de Sartre de 1969 à 1971', *Magazine littéraire*, Nos. 55–56, September 1971, p. 36–47

——————, 'Chronologie (jusqu'au 21 June 1975)', *Magazine littéraire*, Nos. 103–4 , September 1975, p. 9–49

——————, 'Les Écrits de Sartre' (1973–1978), *Obliques* Nos. 18–19, 'Sartre', 1979, p. 335–44

——————, *Sartre: Bibliographie 1980–1992* (Paris and Bowling Green, Ohio, 1993)

Lapointe, F and C, *Jean-Paul Sartre and His Critics: An International Bibliography (1938–1975)* (Bowling Green, Ohio, 1975)

Thompson, Kenneth A, *Sartre: Life and Works* (New York, 1984)

Wilcocks, R, *Jean-Paul Sartre: A Bibliography of International Criticism* (Edmonton, Alberta, 1975)

Sartre remains one of the most studied of French writers and the secondary literature on him is vast. Between 1945 and 1985 some 600 books were published on Sartre and until his death in 1980 between 200 and 300 articles were published annually. In 1979, the indefatigable Sartrean scholar Michel Rybalka stated that an ideal bibliography on Sartre would, even then, have contained between 15,000 and 16,000 references. Below are just a few of the books which cover aspects of Sartre's life and work in more detail.

Biography/autobiography and texts relating to particular periods or aspects of Sartre's life

Sartre (Paris, 1977), tr. Richard Seaver, *Sartre By Himself* (New York, 1978). Text of film directed by A Astruc and M Contat released in October 1976

de Beauvoir, Simone, *La Force de l'âge* (Paris, 1960), tr. Peter Green, *The Prime of Life* (London, 1962). Covers the period 1929–44

——, *La Force des choses* (Paris, 1963) tr. Richard Howard, *Force of Circumstance* (London, 1965). Covers the period 1944–62

——, *Tout Compte fait* (Paris,1972), tr. Patrick O'Brian, *All Said and Done* (London:) Covers the period 1962-72

——, *La Cérémonie des adieux* suivi de *Entretiens avec Jean-Paul Sartre* (Paris, 1981) tr. Patrick O'Brian, *Adieux: A Farewell to Sartre* (London, 1984). Covers the period 1970–80

Bertholet, D, *Sartre* (Paris, 2000)

Boschetti, A, *Sartre et 'les Temps modernes'* (Paris, 1985). English translation by Richard C McCleary, *The Intellectual Enterprise: Sartre and Les Temps modernes*, (Evanston, Illinois, 1988)

Boulé, J-P, *Sartre, Self-Formation and Masculinities* (Oxford and New York, 2005)

Cohen-Solal, A, *Sartre:1905–1980* (Paris, 1985). Edited English language translation, *Sartre: A Life* (London and New York, 1987).

Galster, I, (ed), *La Naissance du phénomène Sartre: Raisons d'un succès 1938–1945* (Paris, 2001).

——, *Sartre, Vichy et les intellectuels* (Paris, 2001)

Gerassi, J, *Jean-Paul Sartre: Hated Conscience of His Century* (Chicago and London, 1989)

Hayman, R, *Writing Against: A Biography of Sartre* (London, 1986)

Jeanson, F, *Sartre dans sa vie* (Paris, 1974)

——————, *Sartre* (Paris, 2000). Originally published in 1955

Perrin, M, *Avec Sartre au Stalag 12D* (Paris, 1980). An account of Sartre's experience as a POW by a fellow prisoner.

Thody, P, *Sartre: A Biographical Introduction* (London, 1971)

Todd, O, *Un Fils rebelle* (Paris, 1981)

Literary Criticism

Barnes, H, *Sartre and Flaubert* (Chicago and London, 1981).

Burgelin, C, *Les Mots de Jean-Paul Sartre* (Paris, 1994)

Contat, M (ed) *Pourquoi et comment Sartre a écrit Les Mots* (Paris, 1996)

Deguy, J, *La Nausée de Jean-Paul Sartre* (Paris, 1993)

Galster, I, *Le Théâtre de Jean-Paul Sartre devant ses premiers critiques* (Paris, 2001)

Gore, K, *Sartre: La Nausée and Les Mouches* (London, 1970)

Idt, G, *La Nausée: Sartre* (Paris, 1971)

O'Donohoe, B, *Sartre's Theatre: Acts for Life* (Berne, 2005)

Reed, P, *Sartre: La Nausée* (London, 1987). In English.

Thody, P, *Jean-Paul Sartre: A Literary and Philosophical Study* (London, 1960)

Sartre's Philosophy

Starting Out

Aronson, R, *Jean-Paul Sartre: Philosophy in the World* (London, 1980)

Levy, N, (ed) *Sartre* (Oxford, 2002)

Priest, S, (ed) *Jean-Paul Sartre: Basic Writings* (London and New York, 2001). Mostly on philosophy but also contains texts on writing, art and politics.

Laing, R D, and Cooper D G, *Reason and Violence: A Decade of Sartre's Philosophy 1950–1960* (London, 1964)

McCulloch, *Using Sartre: An Analytical Introduction to Early*

Sartrean Themes (London and New York, 1994)

Sartre, J-P, *Existentialism and Humanism* (London, 1948)

Warnock, M, *The Philosophy of Sartre* (London, 1965)

Commentaries on specific texts

Aronson, R, *Sartre's Second Critique* (Chicago and London, 1987)

Catalano, J S, *A Commentary on Jean-Paul Sartre's Being and Nothingness* (Chicago and London, 1980)

Catalano, J S, *A Commentary on Jean-Paul Sartre's Critique of Dialectical Reason Volume 1: Theory of Practical Ensembles* (Chicago and London, 1986)

Sartre and Marxism

Archard, D, *Marxism and Existentialism: The Political Philosophy of Sartre and Merleau-Ponty* (Belfast, 1980)

Chiodi, P, *Sartre and Marxism* (Harvester Press, 1976)

Flynn, T, *Sartre and Marxist Existentialism* (Chicago and London, 1984)

Poster, M, *Sartre's Marxism* (London, 1979)

————, *Existential Marxism in Postwar France* (Princeton, 1975)

Sartre and his Contemporaries

Aronson, R, *Camus and Sartre: The Story of a Friendship and the Quarrel that Ended It* (Chicago and London, 2004)

Barilier, E, *Les Petits Camarades* (Paris, 1987). On Sartre and Aron.

Sirinelli, J-F, *Deux intellectuels dans le siècle, Sartre et Aron* (Paris, 1995)

See also de Beauvoir and the biographies cited above.

Sartre and Politics

Birchall, I, *Sartre against Stalinism* (New York and Oxford, 2004)

Burnier, M-A, *Les Existentialistes et la politique* (Paris, 1966)

Drake, D, *Intellectuals and Politics in Post-War France* (London, 2002). Locates Sartre in the context of post-war France and the political stances taken by other French intellectuals. See also Winock.

Lamouchi, N, *Jean-Paul Sartre et le tiers monde* (Paris, 1996)

McBride, W, *Sartre's Political Theory* (Bloomington, Indiana, 1991)

Sartre, J-P, *Colonialism and Neocolonialism* (London and New York, 2001)

Scriven, M, *Jean-Paul Sartre: Politics and Culture in Postwar France* (London, 1999)

Winock, M, *Le Siècle des intellectuals* (Paris, 1997), especially Part Three: 'Les années Sartre'.

Sartre and the Media

Boulé, J-P, *Sartre médiatique: la place de l'interview dans so œuvre* (Paris, 1992)

Scriven, M, *Sartre and the Media* (London, 1993)

La Tribune des Temps Modernes. Commercial release on four audio cassettes of the nine programmes recorded in October/November 1947. Collection *Voix de l'histoire*. Co-produced by INA and Radio France.

A very useful source for material on all aspects of Sartre's life and works is *Sartre Studies International*, a bi-annual publication published by Berghahn Books, 3, Newtec Place, Magdalen Road, Oxford OX4 1RE, UK or 604 West 15th St, New York, NY 10025, USA. The journal is free to all members of the UK Society for Sartrean Studies (UKSSS). For details of membership, please contact Dr Benedict O'Donohoe, Secretary of the UKSSS, Faculty of Humanities, Languages and Social Sciences, Frenchay Campus, University of the West of England, Bristol, BS16 1QY.

Acknowledgements

I would like to thank Sartrean scholar Jean-Pierre Boulé for taking the time and trouble to read the manuscript and for his invaluable comments. I should add, however, that Jean-Pierre is not responsible for the views expressed or for any errors that may have crept into the narrative.

Picture Sources

The author and publishers wish to express their thanks to the following sources of illustrative material and/or permission to reproduce it. They will make the proper acknowledgements in future editions in the event that any omissions have occurred.

Corbis: pp.47, 97; Getty Images: pp. 8, 11, 12, 52, 68, 87, 117, 135; Lebrecht Picture Library/Rue des Archives: pp. 25, 28, 32, 37, 51, 95, 110, 120, 136; Topham Picturepoint/Roger Viollet: pp. i, ii, iv, 15, 23, 54, 78, 83, 84, 90, 103, 105, 106, 112, 123, 124, 128, 143.

Index

Abyssinia, 38
Action, 61, 65
Aden, 24, 30
Africa, 79
Agence de Presse Libération (APL), 1, 2
Alabama, 67
Albania, 43
Alger républicain, 104
Algeria, 55; war of independence, 4,
    96, 99, 100, 101–2, 104–6, 107,
    110–14, 138; human rights in,
    118, 142
Algérie Française, 111
Algren, Nelson, 40, 70, 76
Alleg, Henri, 104
Alsace, 19, 35
Alsace-Lorraine, 9, 49
Althusser, Louis, 122
America, see United States
Antibes, 111
Arcachon, 13
Aron, Raymond, 23–4, 29, 61, 134;
    biography, 24; political involve-
    ment, 27, 35; strained relations
    with Sartre, 30, 68–9; introduces
    Sartre to Husserl, 34; walks out of
    Sartre's play, 67; defends Nizan, 71;
    break with Sartre, 72; attacked by
    Sartre, 125
Aronson, Ronald, 57
Audry, Colette, 39

Auriol, Vincent, 83–4
Australia, 81
Austria, 35
authenticity, 45–6, 60, 69, 87
Aymé, Marcel, 54

Baader, Andreas, 134
Balearic Islands, 31
Barcelona, 43
Barthes, Roland, 122
Bartók, Béla, 76
Batista, Fulgencio, 109
Baudelaire, Charles, 70, 88
Beauvoir, Hélène de, 34
Beauvoir, Simone de, 2, 54, 93, 116;
    relationship with Sartre, 4, 28–30,
    36–7, 40–1, 66, 67, 69–70, 90,
    94, 115, 133; biography, 28; trav-
    els with Sartre, 31–2, 35, 79; and
    Sartre's politics, 33, 90; pre-war
    politics, 38–9; Resistance activity,
    49, 50; in Sartre's company, 52, 76,
    106, 111; claims to have written
    articles, 61; and existentialism,
    64–5; relationship with Algren, 70;
    makes radio programmes with
    Sartre, 72; relationship with
    Lanzmann, 90, 94; wins Goncourt
    prize, 95; visits China with Sartre,
    95–6; and Arlette Elkaïm, 97, 137;
    concern for Sartre's health, 104; and

Fifth Republic, 105; visits Cuba with Sartre, 109–10; visits Soviet Union with Sartre, 114, 118–19; joins Russell Tribunal, 119–20; visits Egypt with Sartre, 121; joins Sartre in television project, 131; reads to Sartre, 132; uneasy about Lévy, 133, 135–7; travels to Portugal with Sartre, 134; death, 137; Sartre's letters to, 139; *Adieux*, 139; *Les Bouches inutiles*, 64; *L'Invitée*, 37; *Les Mandarins*, 95; *Le Sang des autres*, 64

Beckett, Samuel, 52
Beethoven, Ludwig van, 76
Belgium, 46
Ben Sadok, 102
Bergson, Henri, 22
Berlin, 3, 34, 41, 42
Bifur, 30
Blum, Léon, 38, 51
Bordeaux, 49
Bost, Jacques-Laurent, 40, 49
Boston University, 118
Bourdieu, Pierre, 140
Bourg-en-Bresse, 30
bourgeoisie, 20, 24, 32–3, 41, 122
Brazil, 111
Breton, André, 63, 71
Britain, 43, 60, 81
Brittany, 31
Buber-Neumann, Margarete, 77
Budapest, 98

Cahiers du Sud, 54
Camus, Albert, 81; relations with Sartre, 54, 60, 61, 63, 68–9, 75, 81, 82, 87, 107; biography, 55; defends Nizan, 71; death, 107; *L'Homme révolté*, 87, 106
Canguilhem, Georges, 23

Castro, Fidel, 4, 110, 141
Catholic Church, 3, 56, 65
Catholics and Catholicism, 14, 26, 60, 82
Cau, Jean, 67, 92, 93
Ce Soir, 61
Cervantes, Miguel de, 82
Chamberlain, Neville, 43
Chavoix, Élodie, 7
Cherbourg, 7
Chile, 141
China, 4, 81, 95–6, 121
Chirac, Jacques, 131
Churchill, Winston, 67
cinema, 14, 20, 31, 54
class, social, 17–18, 32, 66
Claudel, Paul, 72
Clavel, Maurice, 1, 129
Cochinchina, 7
Cohn-Bendit, Daniel, 124, 125
Cohn-Solal, Annie, 14
Cold War, 4, 55, 141
Collège de France, 117
Combat, 61, 63, 75
Comité National des Écrivains (CNE), 53–4, 61, 65
Comœdia, 53
Conan Doyle, Sir Arthur, 7
Congo, Democratic Republic of, 115
Congrès européene des écrivains, 114
Conrad, Joseph, 22
consciousness, 35, 57–8
contingency, 20, 41
Co-ordinating Committee Against Apartheid, 119
Corneille, Pierre, 11
Cornell University, 118
corydrane, 104, 130
Cuba, 4, 76, 100, 109–10, 111, 113, 141
Curaçao, 76

Czechoslovak Writers' Union, 115
Czechoslovakia, 4, 43, 134, 141;
    Soviet invasion of, 125–6

Daladier, Edouard, 43
Daniel, Yuli, 118, 119
Dayan, Moshe, 121
de Gaulle, General Charles, 24, 49,
    72, 123, 125; resigns, 66; returns
    to power, 104–5; and Algeria, 112,
    113; writes to Sartre, 120
Dedijer, Vladimir, 120
Deleuze, Gilles, 140
Demartial, Georges, 26
Derrida, Jacques, 122
Descartes, René, 22, 100
Doriot, Jacques, 74
Dos Passos, John, 42
Dostoevsky, Fyodor, 18
Dreyfus, Captain Alfred, 10
Drieu la Rochelle, Pierre, 53, 54
Dubcek, Alexander, 125–6, 141
Duclos, Jacques, 85
Dumas, Alexandre, 91
Dunkirk, 15, 46

École Normale Supérieure (ENS), 15,
    21, 22, 23–4, 26, 46, 49, 129, 134
Egypt, 121
Einstein, Albert, 7
Elkaïm, Arlette, 96–7, 107, 118,
    121, 132, 133; as Sartre's heir,
    136–7
Engels, Friedrich, 79
England, 31
Eshkol, Levi, 121
essentialism, 58–9
Euripides, 118
Europe, 42
existentialism, 3–4, 5, 64–5, 70, 71,
    101, 108, 121, 139–40

Fanon, Frantz, 112, 121
Faulkner, William, 42
feminism, 28
First World War, 17
Flaubert, Gustave, 5, 11, 89, 116,
    129–30
Foucault, Michel, 122, 140
France: separation of Church and
    State, 7; pre-war politics, 38–9;
    declares war, 43; German
    Occupation, 3, 49, 53, 55, 58, 61,
    64, 67, 83, 129, 141, 142;
    Unoccupied Zone, 49, 50, 54;
    Vichy regime, 3, 49, 53, 56, 62,
    142; Liberation, 3, 57, 88, 117,
    126, 140; Marxism in, 27, 96;
    anti-Communism, 75; Fifth
    Republic, 105; events of May
    1968, 1, 5, 123–4
France–USSR Association, 93, 99
freedom, 58–9, 64, 88, 122, 140
French Communist Party (PCF), 38,
    74; Sartre's relations with, 3, 4, 33,
    39, 65–6, 70–1, 73, 76, 79, 83,
    85–7, 89, 92–3, 98, 108, 114,
    116, 125, 126; Nizan and, 15, 27,
    71–2; Resistance activity, 51–2,
    65; Camus and, 68–9; Merleau-
    Ponty and, 81; campaigns for
    Martin's release, 83–4; clampdown
    on, 85; and Soviet invasion of
    Hungary, 98; and events of May
    1968, 124, 125
French Resistance, 49–52, 53, 56–7,
    65, 67, 72
French Revolution, 108
Freud, Sigmund, 107, 115, 139
Front de libération nationale (FLN),
    111, 138

Gallimard, Gaston, 40

Galster, Ingrid, 57
Gandhi, Mahatma, 31
Garaudy, Roger, 129
Gaullism, 72
Gavi, Philippe, 129, 131
Geismar, Alain, 128
Genet, Jean, 87–8
Georgia, 114
German Communist Party, 34
Germany, 26, 35; rise of Nazism, 3,
    31, 35; Nazi, 38–9, 53, 77; France
    declares war on, 43; invasion of
    Soviet Union, 51
Giacometti, Alberto, 64
Gide, André, 18, 50
Giraudoux, Jean, 18, 53
Giscard d'Estaing, Valéry, 132
Gomu_ka, W_adys_aw, 100
Grasse, 50
Gréco, Juliette, 2
Greece, 97
group-in-fusion, 108–9
Guatemala, 76
Guevara, Ernesto 'Che', 4, 110

Haiti, 76
Hegel, G W F, 100
Heidegger, Martin, 66
Helsinki, 94
history, 45–6, 49, 108, 122
Hitler, Adolf, 3, 34, 38, 43, 45, 56
Hugo, Victor, 11
Hungary, Soviet invasion of, 97–9,
    100, 114, 126
Husserl, Edmund, 34–5, 42
Huston, John, 107

Indochina, 4, 83, 89, 102, 138, 141
intellectual, role of, 5, 126–7, 140
International Peace Movement, 88,
    89, 91, 92, 99

Ireland, 107
Israel, 69, 120–1, 134, 141, 142
Italian Communist Party (PCI), 114
Italy, 31, 39, 43, 76, 84, 90, 97, 134

Japan, 30, 119, 127
jazz, 76
Jeanson, Francis, 87, 106, 111
Jews, 69, 113, 115, 133
Joyce, James, 115

Kafka, Franz, 115
Kant, Immanuel, 22, 100
Kean, Edmund, 91
Knokke-le-Zoute, 91
Koestler, Arthur, 68–9, 72
Korean War, 81–2, 89
Kosakiewicz, Olga , 36–7, 40, 49,
    83, 94
Kosakiewicz, Wanda, 40, 49, 60, 67,
    94, 106
Kravchenko, Victor, 76–7
Kriegel, Annie, 140
Kronstadt rebels, 20, 21
Krushchev, Nikita, 4, 98, 114
Kyoto, 119

La Cause du peuple (*CDP*), 127, 128
La France libre, 24
La Gauche prolétarienne, 126, 132
La Gauche-RDR, 73
La Revue sans titre, 19, 21
La Rochelle, 16–18, 19, 20, 21, 46
Lacan, Jacques, 122
Lagache, Daniel, 36
Lanson, Gustave, 26
Lanzmann, Claude, 86, 90, 94, 97,
    121
Laon, 40
Le Figaro, 24, 63, 72
Le Havre, 30–1, 33, 34, 35, 40, 41, 49

Le Matin, 12
Le Monde, 101, 123
Le Nouvel Observateur, 135, 136
Le Soir, 15
Lefort, Claude, 88
Léger, Fernand, 63
Légion d'honneur, 61, 117, 138
Lenin, Vladimir Ilich, 21, 27, 79, 88
Leningrad, 114, 115
Les Lettres françaises, 53, 54, 77
Les Temps modernes, 24, 69, 76, 100,
    115; founding of, 3, 4, 64, 70;
    publishes defence of Nizan, 71;
    editorial on Soviet camps, 77; anti-
    colonial stance, 83, 141; tensions
    within, 86, 88–9; attack on Camus,
    87, 106; editorial on Rosenbergs,
    91; stance on Algeria, 101, 111;
    tribute to Merleau-Ponty, 111–12;
    generation of, 140
Lévi-Strauss, Claude, 63
Lévy, Benny, 5, 129, 131–7
L'Express, 104
L'Humanité, 15
Libération, 2, 92, 129
Lindbergh, Charles, 26
literature, 11, 18–19, 22, 42, 93,
    116, 128–9, 139; collaborationist,
    54; of commitment, 70; popular,
    12, 14, 18; Western, 114–15
Locke, John, 100
Loire, River, 30
London, 49, 119
Louis Napoleon, 85
Louis-le-Grand Lycée, 15, 21–2, 23
Lukács, Georg, 75–6, 94
Lumumba, Patrice, 115
Luxemburg, Rosa, 79
Lycée Henri IV, 13, 15, 18–19, 20, 21
Lycée Molière, 40
Lycée Montaigne, 13

Lycée Pasteur, 41, 51
Lyon, 9

Mâcon, 9
Maheu, René, 23
Mallarmé, Stéphane, 139
Malot, Hector, 11
Malraux, André, 50, 69
Mancy, Joseph, 16–18, 21, 66
Mao Zedong, 4, 95–6
Maoists, 5, 126–9, 132, 142
Marseille, 30, 51
Martin, Henri, 83–4
Marx, Karl, 27, 79, 100, 108, 122
Marxism, 5, 32, 68, 73, 79, 81, 139;
    Sartre engages with, 96, 100–1,
    108, 116, 121–2; Althusser and,
    122; reaction against, 141
Mauriac, François, 42, 71
Mayer, Daniel, 51
Melville, Herman, 53
Merleau-Ponty, Maurice, 49, 64, 69,
    72, 77, 79; retreat from politics,
    81–2, 86; resigns from *Les temps
    modernes*, 88–9; publishes *Les
    Aventures de la dialectique*, 94; death,
    111–12
mescaline, 36, 38
Meudon, 8
Mexico, 76
Middle East, 120–1, 134–5; *see also*
    Israel; Palestine and Palestinians
Milan, 111
Miller, Arthur, 96
Mollet, Guy, 101
Morgan, Claude, 53
Morocco, 31
Moscow, 91–3, 96, 114; Show Trials,
    68–9, 81
Munich Agreement, 43
Mussolini, Benito, 32, 38, 43

Nagy, Imre, 98
Nancy, 45
Nasser, Gamal, 121
National Vietnam Committee, 119
Nazi–Soviet pact, 15, 43, 52, 71
New York, 61
Nietzsche, Friedrich, 22
Nizan, Henriette, 30, 63
Nizan, Paul-Yves, 24, 29–30, 61;
  biography, 15; friendship with
  Sartre, 15, 18–19, 21–2, 23, 52;
  political involvement, 26–7, 39;
  death, 46, 52; defended by Sartre,
  71, 73; *Aden Arabie*, 30, 110; *La
  Conspiration*, 42
Nobel Prize for Literature, 2, 55,
  117, 118, 119, 121, 138
North Africa, 53, 76
Nouvelle Revue française (NRF), 40,
  42, 53

Offenbach, Jacques, 29
Organisation Armée Secrète (OAS),
  112, 113

Palestine and Palestinians, 69, 121,
  134, 142
Panama, 76
Papon, Maurice, 113
Paris: Hotel Royal Bretagne, 40;
  Hotel Mistral, 41; German occupa-
  tion, 48–9; Musée de l'homme, 52;
  Café de Flore, 52, 61, 64, 66;
  Théâtre de la Cité, 54, 61;
  Liberation, 58, 61; Saint Germain-
  des-Prés, 64, 65, 66, 76; Les Deux
  Magots, 64, 66; Théâtre Antoine,
  67, 74, 82, 93; Ridgway riots, 84,
  86; Vélodrome d'Hiver, 88;
  Montparnasse Cemetery, 6, 95,
  137; Algerian demonstration, 113;

Sorbonne, 124, 125; Metro, 127;
  Sacré-Coeur, 128; Bibliothèque
  nationale, 139
Parker, Charlie, 76
Pasternak, Boris, 119
PCF, *see* French Communist Party
Péju, Marcel, 86
Perrin, Abbé, 48
Pétain, Marshal Philippe, 49, 55, 56
philosophy, 100–1, 108, 138–9
Plato, 22
Poland, 35, 43, 100
Popular Front, 38–9, 40, 42, 88
Portugal, 134
Pouillon, Jean, 49
Poupon School, 13
Prague, 75, 115, 126
Proust, Marcel, 18, 115

Radical Party, 10, 38
Radio Luxembourg (RTL), 124, 125
Rassemblement Démocratique
  Révolutionnaire (RDR), 73–4
Rassemblement du Peuple Français
  (RPF), 72
Ravel, Maurice, 76
Red Army Faction, 134
Reggiani, Serge, 106
Renault, 124, 128–9
Révolution démocratique africaine
  (RDA), 79
Rey, Évelyne, 94, 106
Reynaud, Paul, 49
Rhineland, invasion of, 38
Ridgway, General, 84, 86
Romains, Jules, 18
Rome, 84, 107, 126
Roosevelt, Franklin D, 63
Rosenberg, Julius and Ethel, 90–1
Rouen, 33, 37
Rousset, David, 74, 77

Russell, Bertrand, 119–20
Russia, 7
Russian Revolution, 16, 20, 21

Sahara Desert, 79
Said, Edward, 135
Saint-Cyr, 29
Saint-Symphorien, 29–30
Sarraute, Nathalie, 64
Sartre, Anne-Marie (née Schweitzer),
     7–8, 10, 13, 14; second marriage,
     16–18, 46; returns to Paris, 21;
     Sartre lives with, 66, 76; Sartre
     gives money, 107; and Sartre's
     autobiography, 116
Sartre, Eymard, 7
Sartre, Jean-Baptiste, 7–8
Sartre, Jean-Paul: birth, childhood
     and family life, 7–8, 10–15, 116;
     impact of father's death, 8–9;
     appearance, 11, 18; reading,
     11–12, 18–19, 22, 27, 129; begins
     writing, 2, 13, 17, 18–20, 89; edu-
     cation, 13–19, 21–2; atheism, 14;
     friendship with Nizan, 15, 18–19,
     21–2, 23, 52; impact of mother's
     remarriage, 16–17, 46; experiences
     in La Rochelle, 16–18, 46; devel-
     ops interest in philosophy, 19; early
     disinterest in politics, 3, 20, 21,
     27, 31–3, 34–5, 38–9; at ENS,
     23–6; gains reputation as rebel,
     26–7, 29, 35–6; love affairs, 27–8,
     34, 64, 90, 94, 115; relationship
     with Beauvoir, 4, 28–30, 36–7,
     40–1, 66, 67, 69–70, 90, 94, 115,
     133; military service, 29–30;
     depression, 30, 35, 36; teaches in
     Le Havre, 30–1, 35–6; early travels
     with Beauvoir, 31–2, 35, 79; atti-
     tudes towards Soviet Union, 4, 32,

67–8, 70, 73, 76–7, 79, 83, 92–3,
98–9, 114–16, 118–19, 125–6,
140–1; relations with PCF, 3, 4,
33, 39, 65–6, 70–1, 73, 76, 79,
83, 85–7, 89, 92–3, 98, 108, 114,
116, 125, 126; attitude to money,
33–4, 106–7; time in Berlin, 3,
34–5; elitism, 36, 48; drug use, 36,
38, 92, 104, 105, 130; relationship
with Olga Kosakiewicz, 36–8, 40;
disinterest in sex, 40, 94; publishes
La Nausée, 40–2 called up and
taken prisoner, 44–8; Resistance
and wartime activities, 49–54,
61–2, 141, 142; engages with politics and socialism, 49–50, 58, 65;
relations with Camus, 54, 60, 61,
63, 68–9, 75, 81, 82, 87, 107; visits America, 63–4, 66; relationship
with Dolores Vanetti, 63, 66, 67,
80; lectures on existentialism, 64;
fame and notoriety, 3–4, 65, 66,
126; commitment, 3–4, 70;
defence of Nizan, 71, 73; breaks
with Aron and Koestler, 72–3;
aligned with RDR, 73–4; thoughts
on ethics, 75–6, 139; musical
tastes, 76; and liberation struggles,
5, 79, 100, 102, 111, 113, 141;
visits Soviet Union, 91–2, 110,
114–15, 118–19, 121; health,
91–2, 93, 105, 128, 131, 134;
diet, 92, 130; visits China, 95–6,
110, 121; engagement with
Marxism, 96, 100–1, 108, 116,
121–2; relationship with Arlette
Elkaïm, 96–7, 118, 136–7; and
Algeria, 96, 99, 100, 101–2,
105–6, 107, 110–11, 113–14, 142;
visits Cuba, 109–10, 113; flat
bombed, 112, 113, 131, 142; joins

Russell Tribunal, 119–20; visits Egypt, 121; dismissal of structuralism, 122; and events of May 1968, 5, 123–5; final break with Soviet Union, 125–6; association with Maoists, 5, 126–9; onset of blindness, 5, 130–1, 132, 134; under influence of Lévy, 132–7; later travels, 134; death and funeral, 6, 137; reputation, 138–43

WORKS: *American Way of Death*, 91; *Bariona ou le fils de tonnerre*, 48, 54, 57, 106, 142; *Carnets de la drôle de guerre*, 44, 45; *Existentialism and Humanism*, 75; *Huis Clos*, 60, 94, 106; *'Intimité'*, 40; *Jésus la Chouette*, 19; *Kean*, 91; *'La Chambre'*, 40, 42; *La Critique de la raison dialectique*, 5, 102, 104, 106, 107–9, 110, 116, 130, 139; *'La Légende de la Verité'*, 29–30; *La Mort dans l'âme*, 76; *'La Nationalisation de la littérature'*, 70; *La Nausée*, 33, 34, 37–8, 40–2; *La Putain respectueuse*, 67, 141; *L'Age de raison*, 44, 64; *'L'Ange du Morbide'*, 19; *Le Diable et le Bon Dieu*, 82; *'Le Mur'*, 40, 42; *Le Sursis*, 52, 60, 64; *'Les Communistes et la paix'*, 85–6, 88; *Les Mains sales*, 73, 74–5; *Les Mots*, 2, 89–90, 94, 115–16; *Les Mouches*, 52, 53, 54–7, 61, 82–3, 106, 142; *Les Séquestrés d'Altona*, 106; *L'Être et le néant*, 50, 52, 57–60, 61, 66, 75, 96, 107, 130; *L'Idiot de la famille*, 130; *L'Imaginaire*, 36; *'Matérialisme et révolution'*, 68, 71, 108; *Morts sans sépulture*, 67; *Nekrassov*, 93; *'Présentation des Temps modernes'*, 70; *'Qu'est-ce que la littérature'*, 4, 70; *'Questions de méthode'*, 100, 102, 108; *Réflexions sur la question juive*, 69; *Roads to Freedom*, 3, 44, 52, 76, 130; *Saint Genet, comédien et martyre*, 87–8; *The Trojan Women*, 118; *The Witches of Salem*, 96

Schopenhauer, Arthur, 22
Schweitzer, Albert, 9
Schweitzer, Auguste, 9
Schweitzer, Charles (Karl), 9–10, 13, 14, 21
Schweitzer, Georges, 7, 16
Schweitzer, Louis, 9
Schweitzer, Louise (née Guillemin), 9–10, 13, 14; influence on Sartre, 18, 20; death, 30
Second World War, 2, 3, 5
Sens, Simone-Camille, 27–8
SFIO, 27, 38, 51, 73
Sholokhov, Mikhail, 119
Sino-Japanese War, 31
Sinyavski, Andrey, 118, 119
Solzhenitsyn, Alexander, 118–19, 141
Soviet Union, 69, 74; Sartre's attitudes towards, 4, 32, 67–8, 70, 73, 76–7, 79, 83, 92–3, 98–9, 114–16, 118–19, 140–1; German invasion of, 51; camps in, 76–7, 79, 141; Merleau-Ponty and, 81–2; Sartre visits, 91–2, 110, 114–15, 118–19, 121; invasion of Hungary, 97–9, 100, 126; liberalization in, 116; invasion of Czechoslovakia, 125–6; Sartre breaks with, 125–6; repression in, 134; *see also* Nazi-Soviet pact
Soviet Writers' Union, 119
Spain, 31, 39, 40, 50, 95, 134
Spanish Civil War, 39, 40, 50
Stalin, Joseph, 85, 88, 97
Stendhal, 18
Stéphane, Roger, 77

Stern, Mikhail, 134
Stockholm, 91, 120
Strasbourg, 44
Stravinsky, Igor, 76
structuralism, 122, 139
Stuttgart, 134
Sudetenland, 43

Third World, 115, 121, 125
Thiviers, 7, 8, 27
Tito, Marshal Josip, 4, 76, 79, 110
Todd, Olivier, 140
Tokyo, 119
Tolstoy, Leo, 19
torture, 101–2, 104, 105, 142
Toulon, 7
Toulouse, 28
Tribune des Temps modernes, 72, 73
Trier, 46
Trotsky, Leon, 74
Tunisia, 50
Turkey, 81
Twórczo, 100

Ukraine, 134
UNESCO, 23
United States, 61, 69, 81, 92, 141;
    Sartre visits, 63–4, 66; racism in,
    67, 79, 141; trade unions, 74; State
    Department, 77; foreign policy, 83;
    imperialism, 111; and Vietnam, 5,
    118

University of Jerusalem, 134

Valéry, Paul, 22
Valois, Georges, 15
Vanetti, Dolores, 63, 66, 67, 69–70,
    80
Venice, 90
Vernier, Jean-Claude, 1, 2, 129
Vian, Boris, 64, 84
Vian, Michelle, 64, 67, 84, 90, 94,
    97
Vichy, 49
Vienna, World Congress for Peace,
    88, 93–4
Vietnam, 5, 83, 100, 118, 119
Vietnamese boat people, 24, 134,
    142
Voice of America, 63
voodoo, 76

Warsaw, 100
Welles, Orson, 63
Wittgenstein, Ludwig, 12
working class, 33, 70–1, 73, 86, 88
Wright, Richard, 67

Young Socialists, 20
Yugoslavia, 4, 79, 97, 110, 141

Zévaco, Michel, 12
Zola, Émile, 10
Zonina, Léna, 115